Understanding
Misunderstandings

Understanding Misunderstandings
Exploring Interpersonal Communication

ROBERT SHUTER
Marquette University

HARPER & ROW, PUBLISHERS
New York   Hagerstown   San Francisco   London

Illustrations created by Robert Shuter

Sponsoring Editor: James B. Smith
Project Editor: Brigitte Pelner
Designer: Helen Iranyi
Production Supervisor: Marion A. Palen
Compositor: Kingsport Press
Printer and Binder: The Murray Printing Company
Art Studio: The Quinlan Artwork Company, Ltd.

UNDERSTANDING MISUNDERSTANDINGS:
Exploring Interpersonal Communication

Library of Congress Cataloging in Publication Data

Shuter, Robert.
    Understanding misunderstandings.

    Bibliography: p.
    Includes index.
    1. Interpersonal communication.   I.   Title.
BF637.C45S54   301.1   78–8012
ISBN 0–06–046132–2

To my parents, Louis and Sylvia, who taught me the real meaning of love, understanding, and commitment.

Contents

CHAPTER 11

UNDERSTANDING MISUNDERSTANDINGS: PRACTICING WHAT'S BEEN
PREACHED   179

Preface

According to educational psychologists, individuals tend to read and retain material that is understandable, stimulating, and applies, in some way, to their lives. With this in mind, I decided several years ago to write a book on interpersonal communication that had these elements. To accomplish this, several unique features were included in *Understanding Misunderstandings.*

First, the book is replete with case studies, each a vivid description of a communication encounter. The cases illustrate theoretical concepts presented in a chapter. What's more, they demonstrate how these concepts can be applied to interpersonal situations.

To stimulate additional interest, unexamined case studies, interpersonal exercises, and suggested projects are included at the end of each chapter. This feature presents the reader with another opportunity to apply theory to interpersonal relationships.

Finally, while writing the book, I was particularly concerned about readability; clarity, interest, and liveliness are stylistic goals I worked hard to achieve.

In acknowledging the contributions of others, I would especially like to thank my wife, Diana—who served as my principal critic— for providing invaluable editorial assistance and for responding supportively when I needed it most; Glen Guszkowski for sketching the initial illustrations; Bill and Joyce Galya for insightful evaluation of the illustrations; the reviewers for helpful commentary; Ann Ludwig, Ronald Taylor, Brigitte Pelner, and James Smith for editorial guidance; Sue Clinton for typing the text; my students for encouraging the completion of the manuscript; the administration at Marquette University for providing an academic environment which enabled me to thrive as a teacher and researcher; and the people who appear in the case studies for supplying me with interesting encounters about which to write.

CHAPTER 1

In the Beginning
There Was Communication

We are always communicating; we have no choice. Each time we engage a friend or stranger in a conversation, communication takes place. Our recognition of objects, people, sounds, and odors is a form of communication. Why, we even communicate with ourselves. Communication is a continuous process; in fact, we take part in literally thousands of interactions each and every day. Confused? Read on.

COMMUNICATION:
A CONTINUOUS PROCESS

Strange as it may seem, communication is simply the transfer of meaning between two people (*interpersonal* communication) or a person and the environment (*environmental* communication). In addition, dreams, thinking, and other self-reflective activities are examples of *intrapersonal* communication, for meaning is transferred within the human being.

For example, during interpersonal communication, meanings are conveyed through words, body movements, physical characteristics, apparel, even smells. Similarly, we communicate with our environment whenever we identify that which we experience, be it a book in the library or a no-smoking sign. And during those pensive moments, while deep in thought, we are, in a very real sense, communicating with ourselves. In short, underlying interpersonal, environmental, and intrapersonal communication is the act of bringing meaning to objects, people, words, and ideas—all our sensory experiences.

Apparently, each time we impose meaning on the world in which we live, communication takes place. To better understand this abstract view of communication, consider the many transactions you might engage in during a visit to the dentist for a yearly checkup.

Dental Dread

If you're like me, you probably worry more and more about a dental appointment as the painful hour approaches. You may even debate with yourself whether you should cancel the appointment, a common *intrapersonal* argument for a dental coward.

With the arrival of the fateful day, you reluctantly proceed to the dentist's office. Upon entering, you are confronted by objects, sounds, and smells— an occasion for much *environmental* communication. In fact, the shrill noise of the high-speed drill and muffled cries of the patient communicate quite clearly that this is not going to be a pleasurable experience. After noticing that the receptionist is calling you, your first *interpersonal* transaction, you realize it is your turn.

While walking slowly into the dentist's inner office, you wonder just how many cavities you have, a common intrapersonal communication. On seeing the expensive dental equipment, another environmental transaction, you conclude that Dr. Smith will probably try her best to find a few cavities.

It appears, then, that we cannot not communicate. Everything we experience, from the words on this page to a muffled cry, is a potential message. Surrounded by an infinite number of verbal and nonverbal stimuli—language, objects, people, and odors—we are communicating continuously. What's more, we interpret messages in a personal way. Consider the following.

COMMUNICATION IS PERSONAL

New in town, you have just met several individuals who urge you to join them for a drink at a local disco. Like yourself, the new acquaintances are male and in their early twenties. So you willingly accept the offer.

Upon entering the disco, you immediately notice that the brightly illuminated dance floor is packed with people, some of whom are dancing alone, while others are paired with individuals of the same sex. Needless to say, the gyrating male couples stand out prominently.

After a short wait your group is seated near the dance floor. No sooner do the drinks arrive when one of your new "friends" politely asks you to dance. What's your first thought?

As an American, you would probably conclude that either the atmosphere was unusually gay or your friends were. All things considered, a verdict of homosexuality would have been rendered. However, your evaluation could be no further from the truth.

You see, the preceding scene took place in Paris, France. In this culture, "straight" males sometimes dance with one another if they happen to be friends. Because you were taught by your American parents that "real" men do not dance together, you naturally assumed the Frenchman was a homosexual. However, this interpretation was an American one.

The vignette demonstrates that the backgrounds of individuals greatly influence the way they interpret a message (see figure). In the preceding case, for example, cultural conditioning was primarily responsible for the erroneous evaluation. Moreover, a person's attitudes and ethnic background significantly affect the interpretation of verbal and nonverbal signals. With this in mind, it should come as no surprise that people raised in diverse environments often perceive the same message quite differently.

To be sure, human communication is both personal and complex. Not only is everything we experience a potential message, but the interpretation of this information often varies from person to person. As you read on, you will certainly wonder how we ever manage to get our messages across.

The Personal Jigsaw Puzzle: A Transactional Approach to Communication

Reality can be compared to one large jigsaw puzzle in disarray. To make sense out of this puzzle, we label the pieces; that is, we assign meanings to all we experience.

As demonstrated, we learn the meaning of these puzzle pieces through past experience, particularly from the society in which we were raised. Without these meanings, we would not be able to understand people, words, objects, or sounds—the pieces of our reality puzzle. In short, it is through communication—the process of assigning meaning—that reality becomes intelligible for us.

In emphasizing the personal, subjective nature of meaning transfer, I am describing the transactional approach to communication, an approach that can be easily applied to our daily interactions.[1] Reflect on the following case, for example.

Sitting in political science class, Nopo, a recent exchange student from Nigeria, listened intently to the professor discuss power. While taking very careful notes, Nopo heard his professor refer to what he thought was a new type of power.

"Some presidents use the power of office to persuade," observed the professor. "Others use the power of words. Still others employ bullshit forms of power to govern."

Unfamiliar with the term bullshit, Nopo assumed it was the name of a legitimate theory of leadership. Interested in finding out more about "bullshit power," Nopo raised his hand and asked quite seriously,

"Professor Jones, your bullshit theory interests me. Could you give me any examples of the bullshit that you speak of?"

Pandemonium broke loose; students laughed hysterically, literally rolling into the aisles. The professor, however, did not find the statement very humorous. After the class quieted down, Jones sternly said, "Mr. Nopo, you've wasted class time with your offensive sense of humor. If you want to debate the merits of my theory with me, see me after class."

Thoroughly confused, Nopo couldn't figure out what he had done wrong.

CASE ANALYSIS. From a transactional perspective, Nopo and the professor were guilty of interpreting a piece of the human puzzle in their own ways. In Nopo's case, he naturally assumed "bullshit power" was a respectable concept since, in his culture, professors are revered and never curse in class. Unaware of Nopo's interpretation of the word, the professor concluded that the student was attempting to embarrass him. It seems that the characters' personal interpretations of language were inaccurate.

Though the situation is humorous, don't laugh too hard at the participants for you also interpret reality in a personal way. Remember the last time you failed an exam because you misunderstood the directions? How about the run in you had with your boss after you misinterpreted his orders? And then there was the fight with your beloved when you mistakenly thought he/she was insulting you. In each case, you imposed the wrong meaning on a particular message because you interpreted it the only way you could—your own way. Once you realize that individuals experience reality in a personal way—imposing their *own* meanings on environmental and interpersonal messages—it should come as no surprise that people often misunderstand one another.

An awareness of the transactional approach to communication, then, makes misunderstandings understandable. So don't forget the approach; it will come in handy in each and every section of this book.

Now that we have established what communication is, let's begin examining the main topic of this book, interpersonal communication.

INTERPERSONAL COMMUNICATION: AN INTRODUCTION

Can you imagine what it would be like to have committed a crime for which solitary confinement was the punishment? Unable to share your thoughts and feelings with others, your sanity might slowly slip away. Craving human contact, you would dream about past relationships and fantasize about those in the future. To escape the loneliness, your new companions might be roaches, bedbugs, even inanimate objects. Deprived of human communication, life itself might not be worth the effort.

Like food and water, we need interpersonal communication to survive. Communicating with others is so important that each of us could stand to learn much more about the process. For starters, let's take a look at some of the basics of communication through the following case.

With exam week approaching, I decided to attend an open house party—a final fling before a difficult test, my last as an undergraduate. Interested in meeting a female that evening, I dressed in my most provocative attire—bib overalls and gym shoes. Proud of my appearance, I went to the party.

Upon entering the apartment, I scanned the room in search of a familiar face. Through the smoke I caught a glimpse of an attractive woman who seemed to be looking in my direction. Realizing I was being watched, I assumed a cool male posture, characterized by casually leaning against the wall, seemingly uninterested in husseling. Appearing aloof, she also attempted to conceal her interest in me, though occasionally our eyes met.

Believe it or not, the two of us spent the entire evening "posing" for each other; nobody was willing to make the first move. However, several weeks later I did meet her, and eventually she became my wife.

CASE ANALYSIS: UNFOCUSED AND FOCUSED INTERACTION. Despite our reluctance to speak that evening, the two of us communicated quite a bit with each other. For example, after observing my wife's physical appearance from across the room, I could tell she was raised in an upper middle class home. Dressed in the latest apparel, her body movements controlled and sophisticated, I guessed she was a business administration or psychology major. On the basis of my appearance, my wife informs me that she thought I was a lost sociology or philosophy student in search of my identity. Apparently, the "cool" body posture I assumed did not convey a very favorable impression. Long before we formally acknowledged each other, the two of us were communicating vis-a-vis our body movements and clothing, an example of what Erving Goffman calls *unfocused interaction*.[2]

Most interpersonal communication is of an unfocused nature. It occurs whenever we observe and/or listen to an individual with whom we are not formally conversing. It takes place in crowded elevators, buses, and trains as the inhabitants glance rapidly at one another. It happens in classrooms whenever the students inconspicuously "read" the apparel, hair length, and body movements of their peers while categorizing those classmates as freaks, jocks, greasers, and straights. Why, unfocused interaction is the backbone of "people watching," for without ever speaking to an individual we speculate on a person's ethnic background, socioeconomic status, political ideology, even sexual preference. To bring this concept home, let's do a little unfocused interacting now!

Select a nearby person and watch him/her closely without the individual being aware of your presence. Eyeball his/her shoes, socks, pants, and shirt, noticing both fit and style; does the attire communicate anything to you? Now look at his/her body, and pay particular attention to height, weight, and build; are these additional sources of information? If your subject is talking, try to listen to the conversation while also observing his/her gestures and other bodily movements; what new conclusions have you derived?

By this time, you have probably collected quite a few impressions of your subject. However, because all your information was acquired on the sly, your observations cannot be easily validated. Unless you engage the individual in a face to face conversation, commonly called a *focused interaction*, you will never know whether your unfocused evaluation was accurate.

A Head On Rap: Focused Interaction

Unlike an unfocused interaction, both participants in a focused encounter realize they are communicating with each other.[3] Standing about three feet apart and looking directly at one another, focused communicators knowingly send and receive both verbal and nonverbal messages. It is the type of person-to-person communication with which we are most familiar.

Just reflect for a moment on your past focused encounters; remember how they started? If you are a keen observer, you probably noticed that the transaction was initiated when your eyes met those of another person. In fact, when a potential conversant refused to look you in the eyes, the encounter never materialized. Eye contact, then, plays a vital role in focused interaction; for example, consider your classroom encounters.

If you are like most students, you instinctively avoid the instructor's eyes whenever a question is asked that you cannot answer. A most effective strategy, it frequently prevents any direct conversation between the student and the professor.

Similarly, when you want to terminate a conversation with a professor or, for that matter, any communicator, you normally reduce the amount of eye contact in which you have been engaging. This reduction in eye involvement signals to your partner that the focused encounter is closing. Hence, eye contact is also instrumental in ending a face-to-face interaction.

Now that you are familiar with focused and unfocused interaction, you are ready to examine the communication process: Who talks to whom about what?

BEES ALL: A LOOK AT INTERPERSONAL SIMILARITY

Each of us is very much like a bee. Seeking individuals with whom to communicate, we buzz from person to person, attracted most by those who promise a sweet payoff. Unlike bees, our nectar is interpersonal similarity—the common interests, backgrounds, even attitudes we share with people. It is that which attracts us most to others, the sweet payoff for which we are all looking. To illustrate this, consider the following.

A Hive Analysis

Let's examine your hives, including the institutions of which you are a member and the people with whom you've established a relationship. Beginning with the nuclear family, your most important hive, reflect on your communication with the other members.

If you look closely at this group, you will discover that you interact most effectively with family members who have attitudes, interests, and values much like your own. Conversely, you probably experience difficulty relating to close relatives who do not share your perspective of the world. You may even avoid communicating with your mother, father, sister, or brother simply because you disagree on many issues.

In addition, marital experts have found that nuptial bliss is also influenced by interpersonal similarity. They have discovered, for example, that enduring unions frequently consist of individuals with common interests, attitudes, and values. Furthermore, many marriages that end in divorce are composed of partners who are not very much alike. Evidently, the notion that "opposites attract" is

most likely a myth that was probably first circulated by a greedy divorce lawyer.

Finally, in the school setting, interpersonal similarity significantly influences your choice of friends and acquaintances. Everything from fraternity membership to roommate selection is based on presumed similarities between yourself and others. Unsurprisingly, those school mates to whom you are most attracted, your best friends, probably share many of your thoughts and feelings.

Accordingly, each of our communication encounters—be it long or short term, marital or friendship—is greatly affected by interpersonal similarity. In fact, research by Wood, Vick, and others clearly suggests that the more individuals have in common, the easier it is for them to converse and establish rapport.[4] No wonder communicators search for commonalities when they first meet one another, and continue this exploration throughout the relationship.

Interpersonal similarity also influences each *stage* of communication—which brings us to another topic.

THE STAGES OF INTERPERSONAL COMMUNICATION

When two people meet for the first time, you can almost predict what they will talk about. In addition to commenting about the weather, the two will probably explore other impersonal subjects of common interest, information normally exchanged during the initial stage of communication commonly called the *phatic* period. The encounter may falter if one of the communicators suddenly shifts the conversation from similar job interests to his/her love life, a topic reserved for a later communication stage.

Evidently, interpersonal communication is conducted in stages, beginning with the phatic period during which surface commonalities and light topics are explored.[5] A highly structured stage, phatic interaction usually begins with such creative openers as "How's things?", "What's up?", "What's going on?", and the ever popular "What's happening?" Only by reaching the personal stage of interaction, the next communicative plateau, can two individuals engage in more meaningful conversation.

In the personal stage, individuals are less reluctant to reveal their feelings. It is a period of moderate interpersonal risk during which both communicators discuss issues of personal import such as marital problems, family difficulties, love affairs, and the like. Only relationships founded on trust ever reach this stage.

Finally we come to the intimate stage of communication. In this period, communicators reveal their innermost thoughts and feelings—their fears and joys, weaknesses and strengths. Marked by intimate revelations, this stage is reserved for individuals who have established a deep union, one based on love, respect, and understanding.

To Phatic or Not to Phatic: That's the Question

Believe it or not, we spend most of our time engaging in phatic interaction. Our daily encounters in the marketplace with employers, fellow workers, garbagemen, appliance salesmen, and others are normally on the phatic level. These conversations are usually limited to a ritualized greeting, a discussion of the business at hand, and a courteous though perfunctory closing: "Thanks much." "Have a nice day." "See you later." Rarely do we disclose or discuss personal matters.

You see, in a society like ours that reveres productivity, personal and intimate conversations are frequently considered wasteful, particularly if they take place in school, on the job, and in other production-oriented settings. In fact, penalties are often administered to those who "waste" company or classroom time by engaging in too many personal conversations. Most of our daily transactions are of a phatic nature whether we like it or not; if you don't believe me, try this:

> Shop in a large supermarket on a crowded Saturday afternoon. After picking up an item or two, saunter over to the check out line. As you near the clerk, try to initiate a personal or intimate conversation with her. You'll find that cute old men will "accidentally" bump into you with their grocery baskets; sweet middle aged ladies will seriously consider assassinating you; and little tots will unabashedly scream ugly epithets in your face—just because you held up the line.

Though phatic communicators by day, we are expected, nevertheless, to soar to personal and intimate heights with our beloved when we return home for the evening. Frequently, it does not work out this way. Consider.

"I Want a Dozen Rolls and a Loving Relationship": Impressions on Synchronized Interaction

Remember the last time you wanted to have a heavy conversation with your friend, lover, or spouse but could not elicit any more from your partner than a summary of the day's activities? You were probably hurt, even angered, just because that person would not elevate the conversation from the phatic level to a more personal level. And then there was the chat you had on a plane, train, or bus with an unfamiliar man who, for some reason, began pouring his heart out to you. Embarrassed and most uncomfortable, you suffered through the intimate disclosures of a complete stranger from whom phatic conversation was expected and appropriate. In both instances, the transaction was unsuccessful because the participants were interacting on different communication levels, a clear case of *unsynchronized* interaction.

As communicators, we have two options: We can either interact with our partner on the same communication level—be it phatic, personal, or intimate—or we can engage in unsynchronized interaction. If we select the first option, otherwise referred to as *synchronized* interaction, we will reap the benefits derived from satisfying each other's communicative needs. However, if for some reason, two communicators find themselves on different levels of intimacy—option number two—frustration, embarrassment, even conflict may result, as demonstrated in the preceding examples.

BOXES, BOXES, BOXES

Exploring interpersonal communication is like unwrapping a gift housed in an infinite number of boxes. With each probe, we uncover unexpected problems and complexities that seemingly frustrate our search for simple communicative truths. And yet, each communication issue must be opened and thoroughly examined before we can reach the prized possession—an understanding of human interaction.

SUMMARY

1. Communication is essentially the transfer of meaning.

    To communicate, individuals must be able to bring meaning to all that they experience, including, among other things, objects, people, words, smells, and sounds. Because many of these meanings are learned early in life, each of us rapidly becomes a communicator.

2. Communication is continuous—a never-ending process with no beginning or end.

    Each of us is constantly receiving interpersonal, environmental, and intrapersonal messages. In sleep, dreams (intrapersonal communication) invade our subconscious. In the real world, people (interpersonal communication) and objects (environmental communication) are rich message sources.

3. Communication is personal, a unique transaction between the individual and that which is experienced.

Because a person's interpretation of a message is influenced by age, sex, race, ethnic group, and attitudes, it can be concluded that communication is personal. Individuals raised in diverse environments often evaluate the same message quite differently.

4. Interpersonal communication can be conducted on a focused or unfocused basis.

An unfocused interaction occurs whenever we observe and/ or listen to an individual with whom we are not conversing. In contrast, both participants in a focused transaction knowingly send and receive verbal and nonverbal messages.

5. Attracted by interpersonal similarities, we strive to communicate with those who are most like us.

Research indicates that the more we have in common with an individual, the easier it is to communicate with that person. Unsurprisingly, enduring relationships generally consist of people with similar interests, attitudes, and values.

6. Interpersonal communication is conducted in three stages: phatic, personal, and intimate.

Light topics and surface commonalities are explored during the phatic period, while more personal data are disclosed in later communication stages. Only relationships based on mutual trust and understanding achieve any level of intimacy.

7. Communication encounters are either synchronized or unsynchronized.

When individuals converse on the same communication level— be it phatic, personal, or intimate—the interaction is synchronized. Conversely, during an unsynchronized interaction, the participants are communicating on different levels of intimacy.

PRACTICE CASE STUDY

Louis has been working for the same company the last fifteen years. Though the firm has not rewarded him handsomely for his dedicated service, Louis still has a special attachment to the job and organization. In fact, he is overwhelmed with guilt whenever he contemplates switching jobs for economic reasons. Why, look what happened when Louis applied for an accounting position at a nearby corporation.

On returning to his office after the clandestine job interview, Louis ran into his supervisor.

"Get to work Louis," the supervisor bellowed sternly. "No goofin' off today or you'll hear from me. Get it?" While the supervisor frequently screamed at his personnel for no reason, today's excoriation was somehow different for Louis.

"My God, he knows," Louis thought. "I can tell from his tone of voice and serious expression that he is aware I may leave the company." Sorry he had ever taken the interview, Louis went to his desk and began working.

Noticing his two colleagues were not at their desks, Louis scanned the room in search of them. Spotting the two accountants at the coffee machine, Louis watched them from across the room as they chattered away.   ·

"I wonder why they're so animated," pondered Louis. "Normally they're as dead as doornails. I'll bet they also know I took that interview."

In fact, the entire day Louis imagined that every office worker knew he had interviewed for another job. Unable to control his feelings, Louis called his prospective employer and removed his application from consideration.

EXPLORATORY QUESTIONS

1. In what way did Louis' attitudes and feelings influence his interpretation of the supervisor's facial expression and tone of voice?

2. What impact did Louis' personal feelings have on the evaluation of his colleagues' behavior?

3. After Louis removed his application from consideration, do you suppose he interpreted the words and actions of his colleagues and boss any differently?

4. Could you analyze this case on the basis of the transactional approach to communication?

5. Do you think this case demonstrates that communication is personal and continuous? Explain.

ADDITIONAL PROJECTS

1. Identify the intrapersonal, interpersonal, and environmental transactions in this case.

2. If you could talk to Louis, what suggestions would you offer to reduce his anxieties?

3. Reflect on the last time you misunderstood a message because communication is personal.

INTERPERSONAL COMMUNICATION EXERCISES

1. Unsynchronized Interaction Exercise
   Unsynchronized interaction can upset a communication encounter. To find out just how upsetting it can be, engage in the following with an unsuspecting person.
   A. While having a superficial conversation with a friend or acquaintance, suddenly shift your contributions from the phatic level to a more personal level by disclosing several intimate details about yourself. Note your partner's verbal and nonverbal reactions.
   B. After several minutes of unsynchronized interaction, ask your partner how he/she felt when you abruptly inserted personal disclosures. Of course, tell your partner you were only conducting an experiment; the person may think you flipped your banana.

2. Communication is Continuous: An Exercise
   To demonstrate that communication is a continuous process with no beginning or end, try this exercise.
   A. Divide the class into groups of four to six members. Every person in the group should jot down at least four descriptions of each of the remaining members. These descriptions should focus on the members' personalities (i.e., John seems to be a happy person; Mary appears to be a nervous person, etc.).
   B. Pass the written comments to the appropriate people in the group. After each person has had the opportunity to privately read his/her descriptions, the members should disclose them to the group. Discuss the accuracy of the written statements, and explore the reasons why each description was selected.

3. Exercise in Focused and Unfocused Interaction
   Does eye contact really determine whether an interaction is focused or unfocused? To answer this question, experiment with eye contact in these situations.
   A. As you approach someone while walking down the street, continue looking at that person until he/she passes you.
   B. While conversing with someone, abruptly look away from the individual. Do not engage in direct eye contact for the duration of the conversation.
   C. Take a trip to the student union; sit down at a table; pick out an unsuspecting individual and stare at that person.
   Carefully note the many reactions you receive in each situation. In class, discuss what you have learned about the relationship of eye contact to focused and unfocused interaction.

NOTES

[1] See Dean Barnlund, "A Transactional Model of Communication," in Kenneth Sereno and Kim Giffin (Eds.) *Foundations of Communication Theory* (New York: Harper & Row, 1970), p. 5.

[2] Erving Goffman, *Behavior in Public Places* (Glencoe, Il.: Free Press).

[3] Ibid., p. 53.

[4] Roy Wood and Charles Vick, "Similarity and Past Experience and the Communication of Meaning," *Speech Monographs,* vol. 36 (1969), pp. 159–164.

[5] Additional information on communication stages can be found in John Condon, *Semantics and Communication* (New York: Macmillan, 1966); and John Powell, *Why Am I Afraid To Tell You Who I Am?* (Chicago: Peacock Book, 1969).

Communication:
Are You Willing to Take the Risk?

Communicating is one of our favorite activities. We talk to the bus driver, chat with acquaintances, and gab with friends. Jaw in motion and tongue wagging, we chatter about the news, our blues, and the groovy Caribbean cruise. Each day, we rap to inform, rap to entertain; why, sometimes it helps us through some real emotional pain. Communication—we couldn't do without it, despite the fact that it's an awfully risky act.

EVER WONDER WHY?
RISK AND COMMUNICATION

Ever wonder why you're tense before a job interview? Ever wonder why you feel a little nervous just before you're about to meet people you are unfamiliar with?

Have you ever wondered why you frequently experience tension before, during, and/or after communicating? The answer is simple: You want to be *accepted* by those with whom you interact. That is, each of us thrives on being liked; no rational individual yearns for rejection. When we are not sure of securing another person's approval—as in the job interview and the encounter with a stranger—we often experience som degree of tension.

In truth, each time we open our mouths we are taking a risk, for we may be rejected. Exchanging ritualized greetings with a stranger, engaging in a conversation with an acquaintance, and disclosing personal information to a friend all require varying degrees of risk. No doubt about it, every communicator is a gambler.

Gamblers All

Ever placed a bet? If you have, you must have been somewhat convinced that a horse, fighter, or baseball team was going to win before you risked five dollars on a wager. Like commercial betting, interpersonal communication is also a gamble; however, instead of money, we are gambling with our psyches. That is, whenever we communicate, we are betting that there's a good chance of being accepted, rather than rejected, by our partner. When the odds for winning another person's approval are against us, we may decide not to interact with that individual.

Do you remember why you refused to tell your boyfriend what was really troubling you? And then there was the attractive woman

at the disco who you just couldn't ask to dance. In each case, you did not communicate because the risk of rejection was too great: Your boyfriend may have thought you were crazy and the female may have declined your offer. Why did you decide these people would not respond favorably to you? Your communication bookies— trust and self-concept—informed you that you might be unsuccessful. Consider the following.

TO RISK OR NOT TO RISK: TRUST AND SELF-CONCEPT

"I want you to feel free to tell me anything on your mind," observed Mr. Miles, Paul's new employer. Hearing this, Paul offered his boss a passing thought.

"Now that you mention it, Mr. Miles, I am a bit concerned that we only get three paid sick days in this company. Any chance this policy may change?"

Visibly disturbed by Paul's comment, Mr. Miles responded, "Paul, this company's sick day policy is a good one. Only weaklings and goof-offs are out more than three days a year. If you're that type of person, I advise you to look for another job."

Do you think Paul will ever again disclose his concerns to Mr. Miles? Probably not, since Paul can't trust him.

Described as "confidence," "reliance," and "expectation," trust, according to Kim Giffin, significantly influences communication.[1] When we trust a person, we expect that individual to respond favorably to us, to accept our strengths and weaknesses. In contrast, distrust implies that we cannot rely on someone for approval; there is a good chance that person may reject us. Unsurprisingly, the more we trust an individual, the more likely we will risk communicating. Furthermore, we disclose personal information more freely to those we trust, according to Morton Deutch.[2] For these reasons, casual and intimate relationships cannot be totally successful unless the participants trust each other.

As demonstrated in Paul's case, people have to earn our trust; everybody cannot be trusted automatically. Some communicators, however, will not trust anyone; accordingly, they are very reluctant to risk communicating with others. Take Russ, for example.

Self-Concept and Communication

Like all nineteen-year-old college sophomores, Russ wants to date coeds. Though he desires to meet females, Russ always has an excuse for not frequenting the local pub, disco, and other havens for hussling: The people are plastic; the girls are immature; studying comes first. On Friday and Saturday nights, Russ can usually be found in the university gym, making time with a basketball.

Reluctant to start conversations with other students, Russ spends most of his time alone. Without a close friend, he has no one to talk to except me, his advisor, to whom Russ periodically discloses bitter, hostile feelings.

One gloomy, Monday morning, Russ decided he had been isolated long enough from his peers. He came to see me.

"Dr. Shuter, I'm sorry to barge in on you, but I've got to talk to you." Distraught and on the verge of tears, Russ whimpered, "I don't fit in at this university. The girls are all stuck up; I don't trust any of them. And the guys think they are super cool. Everybody in this place thinks they are better than I am."

After calming Russ, I asked, "Have you ever really tried to get to know someone on campus?"

"How could I?" he sadly responded. "They wouldn't have anything to do with someone like me."

CASE ANALYSIS. Now do you understand why Russ will not risk communicating? He genuinely believes that nobody could respond positively to someone like him. Feeling insignificant and worthless, it is not surprising that Russ thinks he is inferior to his classmates. Despite his attempts to blame others for his loneliness—"the girls are all stuck-up"—Russ actually isolates himself from the students.

It seems, then, that our decision to communicate is influenced by our self-concept, commonly defined as the way we see ourselves. Russ demonstrated, for example, that people who do not like themselves will avoid communicating interpersonally. Suffering from feelings of inadequacy, individuals with a poor self-concept think everybody sees them the way they see themselves; as a result, they trust no one. In contrast, those who have a positive self-concept are more willing to risk communicating, for they believe many people will accept them just as they are.

Evidently, we must feel good about ourselves before we can communicate effectively with others. Having established this, one question still remains: How did we acquire our self-concept?

Where Did You Come From?
Development of Self-Concept

Imagine how interesting it would be if you could recall every event you experienced and every person you came in contact with while inhabiting this earth. If you could, you would be able to tell me exactly where you came from; in short, how your self-concept developed. Although I can't give you this power, I can guess what you might tell me if you could remember the past in detail.

First, you'd probably describe how the reactions you received from others contributed to the development of your self-concept. You might say,

> "As a child, I was reminded repeatedly by my parents that I was talented, clever, and so intelligent. Relatives and teachers conveyed the same message to me. Before long, I thought of myself in these terms."

Then you might disclose how you unknowingly adopted some of the characteristics of people with whom you strongly identified, another factor that influenced your self-concept. Again, let's hear from you.

> "There were lots of people I really admired and wanted to be like. My desire to be like them was so strong that in certain cases I thought of myself as possessing many of their desirable traits, be it cleverness or sensitivity. I'd like to think that many of these traits became a permanent part of me."

Finally, you might explain how the roles you played as a child and an adult helped produce your self-concept.

> "Reared as a male, I naturally thought of myself as being aggressive and competitive, characteristics little boys are supposed to possess. Like gender, each role I played—that of son, student, worker, and the like—influenced the way I saw myself."

Evidently, self-concept is a product of several factors: the reactions of others, identification with relatives and peers, and role-playing experiences. Taken together, these factors indicate that the single most influential force on self-concept is other people. Research studies seem to support this theory.

For example, Cooley was the first to suggest that individuals see themselves in much the same way as they think others see them.[3] Called the "looking glass theory of the self," Cooley's position was supported by later studies of Rosenberg and Wylie who found that the more convinced we are that others like us, the more we like ourselves.[4] In addition, the reactions of people we identify with significantly affect the development of our self-concept, according to Zander and Stotland.[5] In short, research suggests that without other people there would be no you.

Now that you know where your self-concept came from and how it affects communication, I have another question for you: How much of your self do you actually reveal to others while communicating? Let's find out.

THE YOU NOBODY KNOWS: PUBLIC VS. PRIVATE SELF

How many people get to see the private you—the insecure, sensitive, vulnerable you? Not too many, save your most intimate companions. Instead, most people you come in contact with know the public

you: the confident, competitive, aggressive you who functions relatively effectively on the job, at school, and in the home. Hidden from view is your private world—a world of fears, desires, dreams, and fantasies that you rarely reveal.

Why is the "you" that you present in public often so different than the private you? In answering this question, Erving Goffman argues that people are too concerned about making the best impression to risk being themselves.[6] So they develop a public self—a self that is acceptable to those with whom they communicate—and, in turn, conceal their real thoughts and feelings. To illustrate Goffman's position, reflect on your behavior during a first date.

Are you concerned about making a good impression the first time you date somebody? You sure are; in fact, you try to display language and behavior that appeals to your partner. As a male, you may act more romantic than you really are, appear knowledgeable on subjects with which you have little familiarity, and engage in social amenities that you would rather not do, like opening doors for your date. Similarly, if you are a female, you may present a passive, deferent public self on first dates, a socially expected demeanor for women, even though you may be quite assertive. On a first encounter men and women often display a public self that has little relationship to their private thoughts and feelings.

Our desire to leave the best impression is not the only reason we hide our private self from view. Gerard Egan writes, for example, that many of us will not reveal private feelings "because we are afraid of closer contact with ourselves."[7] That is, each time we disclose our private self to others we come to grips with who we really are, our strengths as well as our weaknesses. Through self-disclosure, we face the possibility of learning about aspects of us we would rather suppress, a fearful prospect for many people.

Finally, men and women who are threatened by intimacy will not let others penetrate their public self. These individuals do not generally engage in much self-disclosure, since it may bring them closer to people.

Evidently, to have a satisfying relationship with yourself and others, each of us should be willing to reveal ourself to those we encounter. For it is through self-disclosure that we partially fulfill our interpersonal needs, which brings us to another topic.

NEEDS THAT NEED TO BE MET

Why speak at all? If interpersonal communication is such a risky business, often causing tension and heartache, why engage in conversation? Despite the hazards, we must interact with others; it is our only way of satisfying interpersonal needs, which William Schutz defines as the desire to be included, loved, and autonomous.[8] Consider the following case.

Jane is a very unhappy college student. Raised in a family where females were seen but not supposed to be heard, Jane is quiet and introverted, so much so that she has difficulty meeting and keeping friends. In fact, she was coldly rejected from a campus sorority after pledging for several long grueling months.

Jane also can't seem to establish a meaningful relationship with a male. Passive and unemotional, she rarely discloses her private self to those she dates, which ultimately turns off her partners.

Finally, Jane feels overly protected by many people, particularly her parents. Mom and dad tell her how to dress, who to go out with, even what classes she should enroll in. Though she would like to politely tell them to stop interfering, she can't seem to find the words.

Frequently depressed, Jane does not seem to know how to improve her life. Can you help her?

CASE ANALYSIS. To help Jane, you would have to motivate her to identify the cause of her depression: an inability to satisfy basic interpersonal needs. That is, Jane does not receive enough *affection;*

she has difficulty satisfying her need for *inclusion*—the desire to be accepted by others; and she feels that she has little *control* over her life. Until all three of Jane's interpersonal needs are satisfied—inclusion, control, and affection—she will remain a very unhappy person.

Like Jane, each of us wants to be loved, accepted, and in reasonable control of our lives; in fact, we spend much of our time attempting to satisfy these needs. The "hazing" you went through to join the fraternity, the early engagement to a childhood sweetheart, and your decision to correspond with a pen pal were all motivated by the need for inclusion and affection. Moreover, you wouldn't be attending college, playing the grade game, and thoroughly digesting the contents of this book if you were not interested in having some control of your life in the future. However, despite your desire to satisfy the need for inclusion, control, and affection, many of you may be unable to achieve this goal.

As demonstrated in the preceding case, a person must be willing to freely converse with others to fulfill interpersonal needs. Introverted individuals like Jane, for example, often have difficulty developing and maintaining relationships, which can prevent them from satisfying needs of inclusion and affection. Frequently unwilling to assert themselves in public, these types of people also do not have much control over their lives.

Since need satisfaction is contingent on open communication, it is safe to conclude, then, that all of us should be willing to express our feelings and thoughts to those we encounter. To accomplish this, we must be somewhat assertive, a characteristic explored in the following section.

ON BEING ASSERTIVE: GETTING YOUR NEEDS FULFILLED

Have you ever wanted to ask your beloved for more affection but, for some reason, you could not seem to do it? How about the time you wouldn't raise your hand in class even though you really wanted to express your opinion? And then there was the year you purchased an expensive life insurance policy just because you could not say "no" to the salesman. In each case, you were nonassertive, thus depriving yourself of need satisfaction—the affection of your partner, control of a sale, and acceptance of teacher and peers. In short, the more assertive you are, the better chance you have of satisfying your needs.

Assertive individuals can freely express their thoughts and feelings to those they meet; moreover, when the need arises, they may do so persistently. Disclosing their opinions tactfully, assertive people can make their positions known without alienating others. A requisite for need satisfaction, assertiveness is not an inherited trait; we learn to be assertive.

In Jane's case, for example, she was taught at an early age that females were to be seen but not heard. Trained to be passive and obedient, Jane frequently had difficulty expressing her needs and desires, particularly to men. Many women experience similar problems because they, too, were raised to be "good" girls: passive, servile, and agreeable.

Unlike females, little boys are encouraged to be assertive; however, all of them do not turn out this way. There are many males who will not readily express their thoughts and feelings. A product of their home environment, these men were not weaned on assertiveness.

Evidently, quite a few people are not assertive enough to satisfy their interpersonal needs. Similarly, these same individuals are often too passive to fulfill their social needs, which can be defined as requirements for living in a technological society, such as a job and an education.

For example, on a social level, we must assert ourselves to secure employment, obtain a promotion, be admitted into college, and land a book contract. Why, a person's very survival depends on the ability to request and obtain goods and services, a goal that demands a moderate degree of assertiveness. It is not surprising, then, that many people are attending workshops to become more assertive.

Developed about 1970, assertiveness training workshops are supposed to assist individuals in fulfilling their social and interpersonal needs. To accomplish this, the workshop has its members participate in role-playing experiences during which they practice, for example, saying no to a persistent salesman, asking the boss for a raise, and requesting more attention from an intimate. Along with role playing, open-ended discussions, public speaking experiences, and lectures are frequently used in a training workshop to increase the members' assertiveness.

In addition to assertiveness training, there are other workshops being offered throughout the country that promise to improve the participants' communication skills. Though many of these programs employ different methods to achieve their goals, they do have something in common: Each is supposedly dedicated to helping individuals become the best possible communicators. Interested in finding out what the ideal communicator is like? Read on.

REACHING FOR THE MOON:
THE IDEAL COMMUNICATOR

Meet Carol Hines. A gregarious woman, she likes being with people and also enjoys her own company; solitude does not bother her. Neither afraid of involvement nor desiring emotional commitment from most people she meets, Carol has established many relationships, both of an intimate and casual nature. A democratic individual, Carol also does not need to control those she communicates with; however, she wants people to seriously consider her arguments.

Empathetic, open, and acceptant, Carol—a person who likes herself and others—is an ideal communicator for many reasons.

In the first place, Carol has a healthy notion of her role in human relationships. That is, she does not fear being controlled, loved, or included in groups, nor does she need to dominate others and establish a deep union with most people she meets. An emotionally stable person, Carol can accept each relationship for what it is, deriving need satisfaction from many types of encounters. In William Schutz's view, Carol is an ideal communicator because she does not demand more need satisfaction from a relationship than it can provide.

Secondly, Carol is open, empathetic, and acceptant, characteristics every successful communicator must have, according to Carl Rogers, noted authority on interpersonal relations. In discussing empathy, Rogers argues that people must try to enter into each other's world and personal feelings and see these as the other person does.[9] An important quality, empathy helps us better understand those with whom we communicate.

Along with being empathetic, the ideal communicator, according to Rogers, must be willing to experience positive feelings toward others—". . . attitudes of warmth, caring, liking, interest and respect."[10] Once we permit ourselves to have these feelings, we can establish a close relationship with those we encounter. Ideally, we should try to accept our own feelings and communicate them openly to others.

Finally, Rogers points out that good communicators should be secure enough to accept people as they are. Writes Rogers,

"Can I (each of us) permit him (another person) to be what he is— honest or deceitful, infantile or adult, despairing or overconfident? Can I give him the freedom to be? Or do I feel that he should follow my advice, or remain somewhat dependent on me, or mold himself after me?"[11]

If you answered Roger's last question affirmatively, you are not prepared to permit others their "separateness," a common cause of a failing relationship. It seems, then, that we must learn to accept people unconditionally—respecting their talents and deficiencies— if we hope to establish enduring encounters.

While the ideal communicator may be easy to describe, it is certainly more difficult to become this type of person. Each of us can only try to be the best possible communicator; in time, we may succeed.

MUST WE COMMUNICATE?

Though we risk part of ourselves each time we interact, we must communicate; we have little choice in the matter. In addition to satisfying our interpersonal and social needs, communication puts us in touch with the world in which we live, a connection we cannot do without. Communication is necessary for our survival; we cannot afford to fear it.

SUMMARY

1. Communication is a risky business.

   Each time we communicate we risk rejection. The fear of rejection can create anxieties, which sometimes prevents us from communicating with others.

2. Our self-concept and the trust we have in others influence our decision to interact.

   Those with a poor self-concept often fear communicating with others. It was also established that the more we trust an individual, the more likely we will risk communicating with that person.

3. Each of us has a public self and a private self.

   The public self is the "you" everybody knows. Hidden from view, however, is your private world—a world of fears, desires, dreams, and fantasies that you reveal only under certain conditions.

4. Through communication, we can satisfy interpersonal needs.

   According to William Schutz, we have three interpersonal needs: inclusion, control, and affection. Individual happiness is dependent on the satisfaction of these needs.

5. Each of us should strive to be the best possible communicator.

   Individuals should attempt to be empathetic, acceptant, and open—characteristics of the ideal communicator, according to Carl Rogers. In addition, successful communicators do not demand more need satisfaction from a relationship that it can provide.

PRACTICE CASE STUDY

Jerry, a freshman at a large state university, is worried that he will not make it through college. A below average high school student, Jerry was told repeatedly by counselors and teachers that he would be better off learning a trade when he graduates from Edison High. He applied to college despite what they said. Now admitted, Jerry fears he is not smart enough to compete with the other learners.

In his classes, Jerry is shy and introverted. Usually seated in the back of the room, he avoids answering questions and does not participate in class discussion. He will not disclose any part of himself to professors and students.

Jerry has almost no contact with students after class. Lonely and frustrated, he is not a very happy individual.

EXPLORATORY QUESTIONS

1. How do you think Jerry feels about himself?

2. Are any authority figures responsible for Jerry's self-perceptions?

3. Why won't Jerry risk communicating in class?

4. In your estimation, what is stopping Jerry from interacting with other students?

5. What should Jerry do to satisfy his interpersonal needs?

ADDITIONAL PROJECTS

1. If you were Jerry's college counselor, how would you motivate him to communicate more frequently with others?

INTERPERSONAL COMMUNICATION EXERCISES

1. Self-Concept Exercise
   The following exercise is aimed at motivating individuals to assess their perceptions of themselves and determine how others perceive them.
   A. Each person should circle the adjective that best describes him or her.

able	dutiful	irritable	paternal
aggressive	elusive	jealous	perfectionist
anxious	fearful	kind	pleasant
bitter	free	lewd	pragmatic
calm	giving	logical	pretentious
certain	gullible	materialistic	protective
clever	happy	modest	questioning
confident	honorable	naive	rational
courageous	hostile	neurotic	realistic
critical	imaginative	oblivious	rebellious
dependable	impressionable	observant	rejecting
determined	insincere	overburdened	religious
docile	irresponsible	overemotional	remote
dreamy	irresistible	overprotecting	reserved

B. Participants should be placed in groups and asked to disclose the adjectives they circled. After each individual has made a disclosure, group members should circle the adjectives that describe each member. The members should discuss their perceptions.

2. Risk and Communication: An Exercise
Communicating is a risky business. To demonstrate this, participate in the following exercise.
A. Interview at least three people. Ask them the following questions. Discuss their responses in class.
   1. Would you be the least bit nervous asking a question in a lecture hall composed of three hundred students? If so, why?
   2. Have you ever wanted to argue with a salesman but, for some reason, you could not do it. What were you afraid of?
   3. Did you ever desire to express deep feelings to someone but were too nervous to do it? Why do you think this happened?

3. Exercise on Interpersonal Needs
To find out just how important it is to satisfy interpersonal needs, engage in this self-reflection exercise.
A. Try to put yourself in the following situations. Identify the feelings you might experience on these occasions. Share your thoughts with another person.
   1. Desiring to meet new people, you join an organization and attend one of its meetings. At the conclusion of the business meeting, you find yourself alone, while the remaining members interact. Unable to locate anyone to talk to, you watch the group enjoy itself.
   2. It's after midnight at the sorority party and all your friends are with someone of the opposite sex who they met during the festivities. Once again, you're alone.
   3. A newlywed, you discover shortly after marriage that your husband considers himself a benevolent dictator. When he talks, you're supposed to jump.

NOTES

[1] Kim Giffin, "The Contributions of Studies of Source Credibility to a Theory of Interpersonal Trust in the Communication Process," *Psychological Bulletin,* vol. 68 (1967), pp. 104–120.
[2] Morton Deutch, "Trust and Suspicion," *Journal of Conflict Resolution,* vol. 2 (1958), pp. 265–279.

3 Charles Cooley, *Human Nature and the Social Order* (New York: Scribner, 1902).

4 Milton Rosenberg, *Society and the Adolescent Self-Image* (Princeton University Press, 1965); Ruth Wylie, *The Self Concept* (University of Nebraska Press, 1961).

5 Alvin Zander and Ezra Stotland, "Studies of Identification," *NIMH Report,* 1964.

6 Erving Goffman, *Strategic Interaction* (University of Pennsylvania Press, 1969).

7 Gerard Egan, *Face to Face* (Monterey, Ca.: Brooks/Cole, 1973), p. 53.

8 William Schutz, *The Interpersonal Underworld* (Palo Alto, Ca.: Science and Behavior Books, 1966).

9 Carl Rogers, "The Characteristics of a Helping Relationship," in Kim Giffin and Bobby Patton (Eds.) *Basic Readings in Interpersonal Communication* (New York: Harper & Row), p. 412.

10 Ibid., p. 410.

11 Ibid., p. 411.

Seeing It Like It Is:
Perception and Communication

"No one could have resisted the woman's amorous advances. That story about needing my class notes because she lost her own was concocted just to meet me. She was certainly requesting more than just the time of day when she asked provocatively if class was almost over. No doubt about it, she desired me."

UNKNOWN JOCK

Convinced he is God's gift to women, our unknown male can convert a female pleasantry like "How are you?" into a bawdy sexual advance. Though the jock is certainly engaging in wishful thinking, you and I would have great difficulty convincing him that he is deluding himself. Like all of us, the jock sees and hears only what he chooses.

Evidently, what we select to see and hear, and how we interpret events, dramatically affects our daily interaction. Commonly called human perception, this process is the single most important element in interpersonal communication.

HELLO OUT THERE:
PERCEIVING REALITY

Picture yourself in a diving bell beneath the ocean peering out at strange flora and fauna. Unable to leave your metallic capsule, you must experience the alien terrain at a distance, passively observing that which surrounds you. Behind the safe walls of the diving bell, the aquatic environment may seem a bit unreal.

Like a diver, we too are trapped in a container of sorts that isolates us from much of the world. Our diving bell is the bag of skin and bones within which lives a thinking, feeling individual. Permanently housed in this capsule of flesh, our only contact with the world "out there" is through our senses which transmit *images* of reality to each of us. These images or sensory impressions are as close as we come to knowing the world beyond our nose.

In truth, the world of events, objects, and people—the objective reality "out there"—is never touched by human beings. Instead, each person lives in a subjective world, one of sensory images and impressions, that is a product of the perceptual process. To illustrate this, consider the following case.

HASH REHASHED: DISSECTING THE PERCEPTUAL PROCESS

Though only twenty-one years old, Harry Schlipper, a college student, could easily pass for someone twice his age. Strongly opposed to premarital sex, Harry boasts to dumbfounded peers that he is a virgin. A hard liner on drugs and alcohol, he is the only male member of the Women's Christian Temperance Union. To top it off, Harry likes to attend "permissive" college parties to convert the heathens.

In fact, one Friday night, Harry went to an open house party planned by several theater majors. Confident that "artsy craftsy" people are attracted to drugs, sex, and perversion, Harry entered the dark, crowded apartment that evening ready to witness a university version of *Deep Throat.* Low and behold, his wish came true, at least that's what Harry thought.

Once inside the apartment, Harry scanned the smoke-filled room, making his first of many discoveries.

"I don't believe it!" Harry thought. "There are three times as many guys than girls at this party. I'll bet anything these women were invited because they are professional nymphomaniacs." After congratulating himself for the brilliant deduction, Harry continued his journey into the land of the amoral.

Spotting a group of long-haired males—a sure sign, according to Harry, that drugs were nearby—he wandered over to the gathering. As he approached the freaks, he noticed that they were crowded around a tray filled with hundreds of colorful aspirin-sized items. Harry watched intently as the students playfully fingered the cylinders, seemingly exhilarated by the experience. Shocked by their behavior, Harry began preaching to a nearby freak.

"I've never witnessed such a disgusting display of pill popping in all my life. I mean, putting all those pills on a lazy Susan is just too much. Don't you people do anything else but get high?"

Unsure whether he was being bawled out by a narc or a nut, the freak responded. "Are you crazy, man? This is a game—a game you idiot!"

"That's even worse," Harry blurted out excitedly. "It's absolutely suicidal to participate in a pill-popping contest. I'm going to save you guys from yourselves."

Pushing his way into the group, Harry grabbed the tray and heaved the contents across the room. Before a riot ensued, the host quickly intervened and escorted Harry out of the apartment.

Several days later Harry learned that the round items on the tray were colored beans not pills. In truth, it was only a game.

CASE ANALYSIS. Though bizarre, the preceding case accurately depicts what occurred in my apartment on April 27, 1968. Dismissing the incident at the time as simply the work of a religious fanatic, I now understand why it happened.

Like each human being, including this chapter's anonymous jock, Harry is a prisoner of his perceptions, unknowingly distorting and misinterpreting that which he experiences. What's more, his sensory impressions of that party in no way corresponded to the actual event. But why?

Selective Perception: How It Works

As demonstrated in Chapter 1, we are bombarded each second by a host of environmental and interpersonal stimuli; in fact, the people, objects, sounds, and smells that whiz by us every moment are too numerous to count. Unable to notice and remember all we experience, we engage in selective perception; that is, we see and hear only some of the available stimuli that surround us. A complicated process, selective perception is significantly influenced by our attitudes, for we seek information that confirms them and dismiss or ignore contradictory data.

In Harry's case, for example, he quickly focused on the long-haired guests and colored "pills," since these stimuli confirmed his negative attitudes about college students. Naturally, Harry did not notice that most of the guests were conspicuously straight and no one was engaged in illicit sexual activity. Apparently, Harry perceived only part of his environment—the part that supported his attitudes.

Turning to research studies, we find additional examples of how attitudes affect perception. For instance, Bem found that policemen tend to notice more violent scenes in a movie than do most citizens because of the cops' attitudes toward crime.[1] Similarly, Hastorf and Cantril discovered that sports fans loyal to a particular team just happen to perceive the fouls committed by the opposition and ignore the errors of the favored squad.[2] Finally, Schulman reported that a juror's attitudes significantly affect the perception of a defendant's testimony.[3]

In addition to attitudes, a person's gender and background also determine what the individual selectively perceives. One study found, for example, that women generally notice the color and design of objects quicker than men do, an indication that males and females perceive reality differently. Furthermore, researchers have discovered that individuals with dissimilar backgrounds—from diverse social classes, ethnic groups, and cultures—notice different things when exposed to the same information. To be sure, our attitudes "select" only some of what we see and hear; background and gender also play a critical role in selective perception.

Certainly, individuals do not consciously engage in selective perception; it is an involuntary response to their environment. For example, Harry was not aware he perceptually avoided short-haired guests, and the women in the preceding study did not purposely focus on color and design. On the contrary, these individuals are much like you and I, for they didn't realize that their attitudes, background, and gender influenced what they saw and heard. Evidently, each of us has amazingly little control of our perceptual process.

You Made the Wrong Interpretation

Strange as it may seem, the way we interpret a message—that is, the meaning we impose on an event, word, or action—is also influenced by our attitudes and background. In terms of our background, it was established in Chapter 1 that we learn the "meaning" of things from our culture, ethnic group, and past experience. With this in mind, we also concluded in Chapter 1 that individuals often interpret the same message much differently. Moving on to new territory, let's focus our attention on the way attitudes affect the interpretation of a message.

In the preceding case, for example, Harry would not have concluded that the female guests were "professional nymphomaniacs" if he did not firmly believe that college students were extraordinarily permissive. Similarly, had his attitudes been different he would not have speculated that the guests were engaging in a pill-popping contest. Accordingly, Harry's interpretation of each message was governed by his attitudes.

One can also conclude from this case that people with dissimilar attitudes may interpret the same information quite differently. For example, if Harry had been sitting next to a typical college student who was also unfamiliar with the game, I'm sure the two of them would have disagreed over what was going on. Convinced that all people in college are not dope addicts, the university student might have figured out that the strange activity was only a game, while Harry's attitudes led him to another interpretation.

Like selective perception, then, we interpret information subjectively. Unable to detach ourselves for even a moment from our attitudes, we have no choice but to interpret events, objects, and words in our own way. In truth, we can never be totally objective, for we are constantly influenced by what we believe. We should not rule out the interpretations of others, since, as human beings, we are all fallible.

ATTITUDES, PERCEPTION, AND COMMUNICATION

Our attitudes not only help select the messages that we see and hear, but they can distort information as well.

Pat is a typical smoker. Unwilling to believe that cigarettes may kill her, she refuses to seriously consider antismoking messages designed by the Cancer Society and other organizations. Whenever concerned friends or relatives tell Pat that she should not smoke, she usually points out that pollution, asbestos fibers, and the like are certainly worse than cigarettes. Finally, Pat rarely notices the Surgeon General's warning printed on each pack of cigarettes. In fact, she thinks it reads "Cigarettes *may be harmful* to your health" when, in actuality, the statement warns that "Cigarettes *are dangerous* to your health."

A classic example of improper message reception, the smoker distorted and/or dismissed information that challenged her positive attitude toward cigarettes. Pat accomplished this by regarding the cancer commercials as more Hollywood melodrama, dismissing her relatives' arguments as ecological nonsense, and, most importantly, distorting the Surgeon General's printed message. If Pat had not modified these warnings, she would have been a very uptight smoker.

Like Pat, each of us manipulates certain incoming messages to safeguard our attitudes. As a Democrat or Republican, for example, we may distort the opposition's platform to sustain our faith in the favored candidate. In addition, to maintain positive attitudes about their children, parents often refuse to believe that their kids were involved in illicit activity, even when reported by teachers and administrators. You see, once we notice and accept information that challenges our attitudes, we may have to change our way of thinking, a most tension-producing moment according to Leon Festinger, noted authority on attitude change.[4] In short, we alter certain messages to avoid the psychological tension associated with attitude change.

Faster Than a Speeding Bullet: Modifying Messages

The mind modifies tension-producing messages so rapidly that the perceiver is not cognizant of what is occurring. Smokers, for example, are unaware that they have converted the Surgeon General's warning into a less serious statement. Similarly, the parents of a convicted murderer rarely understand that their positive attitudes toward the child caused them to minimize the seriousness of his early aggressive behavior. No doubt about it, we are captives of our attitudes.

If you're still not convinced that perception is greatly influenced by attitudes, examine the following section closely, for it clearly demonstrates that our attitudes control us in ways that boggle the imagination.

Self-Fulfilling Prophecy

A recent university graduate, Dewitt, a black, middle class New Yorker, has received his first teaching assignment in a lower class white school located in the heart of Brooklyn. Disappointed with the position, Dewitt reluctantly reported to school to teach what he thought were racist, unruly, illiterate white kids. Despite his negative feelings, Dewitt vowed that these students would receive the best possible instruction from him.

Fearing a chaotic year, Dewitt was convinced he had to appear as tough as possible to maintain order in the classroom; accordingly, he greeted his pupils that first day of class with a scowl. Taken aback by Dewitt's behavior, the students were passive, almost apathetic, the first week of school.

With each passing day, Dewitt realized he was not reaching these kids. After two months, the students' school work, which they rarely completed, was considerably poorer than it was at the beginning of the term. Moreover, the learners' passive demeanor was replaced by aggressive, combative, even hostile behavior. By November, Dewitt's pupils seemed to be as illiterate, unruly, and racist as he had anticipated.

Unable to cope with the pandemonium, frustrated by his lack of success, Dewitt quit the position at the end of the year.

CASE ANALYSIS. Feeling sorry for Dewitt? You shouldn't be, since he was primarily responsible for his students' behavior.

His troubles started the first day of class when he unknowingly communicated to his students that they were supposed to be illiterate, unruly, and racist. Although never stated directly, Dewitt's attitudes were certainly no secret, for they were etched on his scowling face and evident in his treatment of the learners. Moreover, Dewitt looked for student behavior that would confirm his negative attitudes, though ostensibly he wanted to turn in the best possible teaching performance. Despite his desire to be an objective instructor,

Dewitt's attitudes affected his perception and behavior, and he was not even aware of it.

Unsurprisingly, the students sensed Dewitt's attitudes, and they responded by becoming as illiterate and unruly as the teacher had expected. The learners' behavior, was precipitated by Dewitt's attitudes—a case of self-fulfilling prophecy.

Discovered by Rosenthal and Jacobson in 1962, the self-fulfilling prophecy dramatically illustrates how attitudes insidiously control the perception and behavior of both the sender and receiver of a message.[5] As demonstrated in the preceding case, this theory offers three fascinating conclusions:

1. The perception and behavior of a message sender (i.e., Dewitt) is significantly influenced by his attitudes about a person or group.

2. When the sender converses with that person or group, his attitudes are unknowingly communicated to the receiver(s) (i.e., Dewitt's pupils) both verbally and nonverbally (i.e., Dewitt's scowling face and treatment of his students).

3. The receiver(s) of this "message" responds by behaving just as the sender expected, thereby fulfilling the sender's attitudinal prophecy (i.e., Dewitt's pupils became unruly, illiterate, and racist for him).

Though Rosenthal's original studies were conducted in the classroom, the self-fulfilling prophecy is certainly not limited to this setting. Studies have shown, for example, that many professionals, including counselors, psychologists, and physicians, unknowingly induce their clients to behave in expected ways. In fact, whenever our attitudes about a person influence that individual to respond in an expected fashion, an attitudinal prophecy has been fulfilled.

It seems, then, that our attitudes not only determine what we see and hear, but they also affect our relationship with others. Why, attitudes exert so much influence over peoples' lives that it is sometimes necessary to change a person's belief system in order to help the individual communicate more effectively and perceive the world more objectively.

ON CHANGING ATTITUDES, PERCEPTION, AND COMMUNICATION

Over the years, numerous techniques have been developed to modify attitudes. This section examines several of these methods; in addition, it explores the many ways in which attitude change influences perception and interpersonal communication.

Behavior Modification

Since publication of B. F. Skinner's *Beyond Freedom and Dignity*, teachers, counselors, even parents have been using behavior modification to alter a host of attitudes.[6] In essence, this theory maintains that rewards must be used to induce individuals to change their behavior. Once the subject's behavior is modified in return for a cookie, a transistor radio, or the like, the person will supposedly experience an attitude change as well. Presumably, the subject's perception and communication will also change as a result of the newly acquired attitudes. To illustrate this method, let's examine a case in which it was actually used.

Dino, a junior high school student, has once again been caught fighting with his peers. This time he is sent to the guidance counselor to discuss the matter.

During the counselor's brief encounter with Dino, she learns that he will not utilize other methods to resolve disputes because he feels they will not work. To motivate Dino to settle his arguments nonaggressively, a necessary first step to attitude change, the counselor recommends that the teacher reward him with a valued prize each day he does not fight. The counselor hopes that Dino will eventually realize that violence does not solve problems, and thus no longer require a reward to behave properly.

Like many individuals who have experienced behavior modification, Dino's attitude, perception, and communication changed after only a few months, according to his counselor—the source of this story. Not only did he perceive violent acts more negatively, but he related much better to his classmates. No longer compelled to intimidate others, Dino established additional friendships as well.

Certainly, behavior modification is not always as effective as it was in the preceding case. In fact, many investigators doubt that a method based on rewards can permanently change a person's attitudes. They argue that once the rewards are eliminated, the person's old habits will return.

Like behavior modification, the following technique also attempts to change an individual's attitudes, perception, and communication by first altering the person's behavior. Consider.

Counterattitudinal Advocacy

Cajoled by his professor to participate in a long experiment, Sammy, a college senior, is relieved the task is finally over. In fact, when asked to evaluate the experiment, he indicated on the questionnaire that it was terribly boring and tedious. About to leave the laboratory, Sammy is suddenly confronted by his professor.

"Sam, I could use your assistance at the front desk for about a half-hour. I'll pay you five dollars to simply admit students who volunteered for the experiment into the laboratory. Also, I want you to tell each volunteer that the experiment is a most interesting, enjoyable, and profitable experience."

Although Sammy must present a view he disagrees with, he accepts the professor's offer. After completing his half-hour assignment, Sammy is asked once again to evaluate the experiment in which he originally participated. Surprisingly, Sam's attitude has changed, for he now considers the experiment significantly more interesting.

Believe it or not, Sam's sudden attitude change is not as strange as it may seem. According to Festinger and Carlsmith, the researchers who actually conducted the preceding experiment, each of us might respond similarly if we were "bribed" to present a position that was diametrically opposed to one or more of our own attitudes.[7]

Commonly called *counterattitudinal advocacy,* this technique is frequently successful because individuals experience psychological tension when they are *induced* to publicly advocate a position that they privately oppose. Unwilling to cope with this tension, individuals will often reduce it by changing their attitude so that it is more consistent with the position they advocate publicly. Essentially, this is why Sammy found the experiment more interesting the second time he evaluated it.

The success of this technique depends on the size of the reward individuals receive to contradict their attitudes. In an early study, Festinger and Carlsmith found that subjects were more apt to change their attitude when they received a small reward for advocating a position with which they did not agree. In explaining this finding, the researchers argue that a large reward gives the subjects a built-in excuse for presenting a message that contradicts their attitude—"I did it for the money"—while a small reward provides no such justification; the subjects have to accept responsibility for their behavior. Unable to justify saying one thing and believing another, the individuals experience tension which results in attitude change.

A fascinating and rather complex method for changing attitudes, counterattitudinal advocacy can also alter a person's perception and communication. For example, insurance companies have found that individuals who are unfavorably disposed to life insurance will often invite a salesman to their home when offered an inexpensive, complimentary gift. In accepting the gift, the disinterested customer has to appear interested in insurance—certainly a case of counterattitudinal advocacy. As a result, the client often perceives insurance more positively, communicates the newly acquired attitude to friends and others, and, most importantly, buys a policy from the salesman, according to the regional manager of a large life insurance company.

Certainly less ethical than counterattitudinal advocacy and behavior modification, the following method has also been used to change an individual's attitudes.

Brainwashing

Derived from the Chinese word *hsi nao,* which means "to cleanse the mind," brainwashing can radically alter a person's attitudes. It was used extensively by the Chinese communists to "reeducate" the masses after Mao Tse Tung's rise to power. The technique has also been employed widely in the Soviet Union to "convert" political dissidents. The term, however, reached the public's attention in the 1950's with the return of American prisoners captured during the Korean War who had embraced communism while jailed by the Chinese. Though clouded in mystery and intrigue, brainwashing is actually a systematic method for changing attitudes.

According to Edgar Schein, brainwashing is conducted in three stages: unfreezing, change, and refreeze.[8] In the first stage *(unfreezing)* the subjects are weakened both psychologically and physiologically by their captors. Although the methods vary, the individuals are usually inadequately fed, awakened at night by interrogators, and deprived of exercise. The subjects are also placed in a jail cell with those who have been "reformed." Criticized and berated by cellmates, harassed by captors for holding incorrect beliefs, and deprived of sufficient sleep, food, and exercise, the subjects are often ready to change their attitudes within several days.

In addition to being provided with "enlightened" periodicals, the subjects are exposed to acceptable dogma by the captors during the second stage *(change)* of brainwashing. Striving to regain a sense of worth in this hostile environment, the subjects also start to identify with the captors to whom in desperation they reach out for support and consolation. As a result, their attitudes begin changing.

Finally, in the third stage *(refreeze),* the subjects' newly acquired attitudes are integrated into their personalities. The recipients of much support from the captors, the subjects no longer feel alienated, for they now share the captors' views. They are also treated with respect and sensitivity while being guided by the captors through a critical examination of the new ideology. When the reformed attitudes are firmly implanted in the subjects' psyches, the individuals have been successfully refrozen.

Possessing a complex of new attitudes, the converts perceive the world, interpret messages, and communicate quite differently than they did in the past. For example, take Patty Hearst, the celebrated· convert of the Symbionese Liberation Army.

Kidnapped in 1974 by a radical group, the heiress to the William Randolph Hearst estate vilified her parents and country several weeks after being abducted. Once considered a loving daughter, Patty denounced her mother and father as "capitalist pigs" and interpreted the messages they sent to her as "ruling class bullshit." Deeds she previously found immoral and illegal—burglary, destruction of property, and murder—were now regarded as glorious revolutionary accomplishments. Apparently, Patty's perception, language, and interpretation of messages changed because she had been successfully brainwashed by her captors, according to Robert J. Lifton, one of the country's foremost experts on thought reform.[9]

Patty Hearst's newly acquired communication style was reminiscent of the way American prisoners of war interacted after being converted by the Chinese communists. Like Patty, they considered information from America as "imperialist" propaganda, and they also cluttered their language with revolutionary jargon. In some

cases, converted POW's participated in illegal acts once they returned to the United States.

It seems, then, that brainwashing can radically alter an individual's attitudes, perception, and communication. Although most effective, this technique is a coercive one and thus should not be employed.

Dominoes Anyone?

Remember watching with fascination as hundreds of dominoes lined up in a row tumbled to the floor, each striking the other in a chain reaction? Like dominoes, attitudes, perception, and communication are linked closely together (see figure, opposite). As demonstrated, when an individual's attitudes are altered through behavior modification, counterattitudinal advocacy, or brainwashing, perception and communication are modified as well.

PERSECUTING THE TRUTH: A POSTSCRIPT

Throughout history people have been persecuted, jailed, even executed for not accepting the "truth," that is, for not perceiving reality in a certain way. Jews were slaughtered in Spain during the inquisition for interpreting religious dogma differently than the Christian majority. Revolutionaries have been denounced and punished for refusing to accept established political "truths." Even books, plays, and poems have been censored and banned because the author's interpretation of reality deviated significantly from widely accepted perceptions. Until the inhabitants of this planet realize that each person perceives reality differently—that "truth" is a subjective evaluation—they will continue excoriating those who do not share their view of the world.

SUMMARY

1. The images of reality we receive through our senses are the closest we come to knowing the world "out there."

    Relying on our senses for information about the world, we perceive reality subjectively. For us, the world beyond our nose is simply a host of sensory images and impressions.

2. Our attitudes, background, and gender affect the way we perceive reality.

    Bombarded by numerous stimuli, we engage in selective perception; that is, we perceive certain information and dismiss other data. In addition, the way we interpret events, words, and actions is also influenced by attitudes and background.

3. We often distort information that contradicts our attitudes.

Individuals frequently experience psychological tension when the message they receive contradicts one or more of their attitudes. To reduce this tension, perceivers either change their attitudes or attempt to maintain them by distorting contradictory information.

4. In altering a person's attitudes, perception and communication are frequently changed.

Brainwashing, behavior modification, and counterattitudinal advocacy—all attitude change techniques—can also influence an individual's perception and communication.

5. Since each of us perceives reality differently, it is not surprising that events, words, and actions can be interpreted in many ways.

Throughout history people have been excoriated for not perceiving reality in a certain way. Until we realize that each person perceives reality differently, we will continue persecuting those who do not share our view of the world.

PRACTICE CASE STUDY

Yassir and Ahamed are Palestinian Arabs attending college in the United States. Yearning for warm weather like that of Lebanon, they selected Miami Beach for their winter hiatus despite the fact that many Jews also vacation in this resort. Reluctant to communicate with the other guests, the two spent most of their time together swimming and sunbathing. Though isolated from most of the crowd, Yassir and Ahamed were enjoying themselves until they had their first conversation with an American Jew.

While playing backgammon in the hotel lobby, Yassir and Ahamed noticed a group of people observing their game from across the room. As the group neared them, the two began feeling uneasy. They were particularly disturbed when the group stopped directly behind them and a young female spoke while staring curiously at the backgammon board.

"Looks like it's all over for you," she indicated to Yassir.

Surprised by the remark, Yassir quickly responded. "You say that because I am a Palestinian Arab. I have a right to be here; you do not own this place."

Startled, she replied, "I didn't know you were an Arab. What's more, I don't know what that has to do with what I said."

Ignoring the group, the Arabs, visibly disturbed, continued playing the game. And the American Jews walked away totally confused.

EXPLORATORY QUESTIONS

1. What attitudes did Yassir maintain about American Jews?

2. Do you think his attitudes resulted in some form of selective
perception? Explain.

3. In what way did Yassir's attitudes influence his interpretation
of the female's observation?

4. How do you think the Jewish group interpreted Yassir's angry
response?

5. Do you think the group members' attitudes toward Arabs could
have influenced their interpretation of Yassir's response?

6. In what way did the characters' cultural backgrounds influence
their interpretation of the messages?

ADDITIONAL PROJECTS

1. If you witnessed the preceding incident, how could you have
mediated the crisis?

2. Speculate on how behavior modification, brainwashing, and/or
counterattitudinal advocacy could be used to change the characters' attitudes.

3. In what way have interpersonal misperceptions significantly affected foreign policy negotiations between Arabs and Israelis?

INTERPERSONAL COMMUNICATION EXERCISES

1. Selective Perception Exercise
   Each of us perceives reality just a little bit differently. To demon-
   strate this, participate in the following exercise.
   A. The class should visit the student union. Once inside, each
      learner should attempt to remember most of what is seen
      and heard.
   B. On returning to the classroom, the students should jot down
      their perceptions. Discuss the varying lists and the reasons
      for the perceptual differences.

2. Interpretation Exercise
   The interpretation of an event or word often varies from person
   to person. This is demonstrated in the exercise that follows.

A. Examine the illustration below and write down what you think is happening.

B. In a small group of three to five members, discuss your interpretation and those of the other individuals. Consider how each member's background influenced the interpretation of the picture.

3. Attitudes and Perception: Two Exercises
To say that attitudes control perception is easy; to prove it is more difficult. The following exercises may convince you that attitudes influence perception.

Exercise One

A. Have the cigarette smokers in the class identify themselves. Ask them to write down the *exact* warning that appears on a cigarette pack. For comparison purposes, nonsmokers should also jot down the warning.

B. Beginning with the smokers, each class member should read the written warning aloud. Note and discuss any differences between the students' warnings and that which appears on a pack of cigarettes. Also determine whether the written warnings of smokers or nonsmokers are more accurate.

Exercise Two

A. Remember the last time you were stopped by a cop for speeding? I want you to simulate that event with another person. Each of you should have the opportunity to play the part of the defensive driver and aggressive cop. A third person should observe the simulations noting the different ways the roles are enacted.

B. After completing the simulations, discuss how each of you enacted these roles. What effect did attitudes have on the enactment of the roles?

Notes

[1] Daryl Bem, *Beliefs, Attitudes, and Human Affairs* (Belmont, Ca.: Wadsworth, 1970).

[2] Albert Hastorf and Hadley Cantril, "They Saw a Game: A Case Study," *Journal of Abnormal and Social Psychology*, vol. 49 (1954), pp. 129–134.

[3] Albert Schulman, "Recipe for a Jury," *Psychology Today*, Summer (1972), pp. 42–46.

[4] Leon Festinger, *Cognitive Dissonance Theory* (Evanston, Il.: Harper & Row, 1957).

[5] Robert Rosenthal and Lenore Jacobson, *Pygmalion in the Classroom* (New York: Holt, Rinehart and Winston, 1968).

[6] B. F. Skinner, *Beyond Freedom and Dignity* (New York: Knopf, 1971).

[7] Leon Festinger and John Carlsmith, "Cognitive Consequences of Forced Compliance," *Journal of Abnormal and Social Psychology*, vol. 58 (1959), pp. 203–210.

[8] Edgar Schein, *Coercive Persuasion* (New York: Norton, 1961).

[9] Lifton served as a defense witness for Patty Hearst. See Robert Lifton, *Thought Reform and the Psychology of Totalism* (New York: Norton, 1961).

A Word About Words

Words, words, words; we can't escape them. They beckon you and me to have a coke, wheedle us to munch on a Big Mac, and seduce the populace to buy a Buick. Words promise listeners that the weather will be fair and pleasant; they inform the public that gonorrhea is contagious; why, words even make us laugh. Everywhere we turn there are words, instructing us, commanding us, offending us, thrilling us. To be sure, words put us in touch with the world beyond our nose; we couldn't do without them!

GETTING HIGH ON WORDS:
THE REAL DOPE ON LANGUAGE

All together now, say joint. Say it again, slower and softer; I wouldn't want you to get arrested. Now tell me, what is a joint?

"Good stuff from Columbia," you say.

"What most students deeply inhale before history class, biology, physics, sociology, communication, anthropology . . . ," a few of you exclaim, while munching incessantly.

"Dope," you say. "It can ruin your life, your mind, and your body," proclaims the law enforcement major in your midst.

Believe it or not, you're all wrong. The word joint is not a dreamy drug; it is only a collection of sounds. That is, each of the five letters in this word has a certain sound, the sum of which constitutes the word joint. Like every word in the English language, joint, then, is nothing more than sounds.

"Ain't no way people can get high on sounds," you say. You're perfectly right, for words are also symbols. That is, each collection of sounds—otherwise called a word—has been associated with an object or concept. For example, the j/oi/n/t sounds were, for some reason, linked to a substance derived from Indian hemp; the word roach-clip was arbitrarily associated to a special "cigarette" holder; and the term "narc" strikes fear in many college students because it refers to a type of police officer.

Simply put, a word is merely a group of sounds to which an object or concept has been linked. How and when do we learn what a term stands for, what it means? To answer this, let's take a trip back in time.

THE TIME CAPSULE: LEARNING LANGUAGE

Do you remember much about your life when you were three weeks old? Probably not, since you were barely cognizant of what was happening around you. Lying in your crib, you made few sounds, save an occasional grunt, groan, and ear-piercing howl. If you recall, your parents were upset that you didn't seem to recognize them. Why, they received a warmer response from the family dog.

Appearing detached from the world, you remained this way until you were about seven weeks old, when suddenly you began to react more to people and objects in the environment. Now at the babbling stage, commonly called the *lallation period,* you goo-gooed and gah-gahed your parents crazy. Sensing you might be on the verge of saying your first word, mom and dad encouraged you to speak: "Say mama, say dada; talk, you brat." However, all they received from you was a smile, a great deal of saliva, and more babbling. Though frustrated, your parents didn't give up; you still received daily language lessons.

Then it happened. Your mother was feeding you one day when suddenly your mouth opened wide, pablum rushed out and with it came your first word: "mama." Stunned, mother prompted you to say it again and sure enough you did. Able to *imitate* others— the basis of language learning—you said several words at one year old, the age of linguistic enlightenment.

At a year and a half, you were already expressing yourself in one word sentences—"No," "More," "Mine"—which you also learned by imitating others. By two, prepositions, pronouns, and adjectives appeared in your speech. Capable at three of *inferring* the meaning of words you heard frequently, a step beyond mere imitation, your vocabulary increased rapidly. With the celebration of your fifth birthday, the basic structure of language, its meanings and sounds, was familiar to you.

Certainly, your language development did not stop at five years old. On the contrary, you continued learning the meaning of words inferentially and didactically, two processes that warrant additional consideration.

"What's That?": Didactic and Inferential Approaches to Acquiring Language

W. C. Fields I'm not. Still, there is a lot of truth in what he said about kids; they can be a nuisance. For example, take my six year old nephew Brad— please!

Last year, my wife and I had the distinct pleasure of having this neurotic nerd as a house guest while my sister vacationed in Florida. A curious kid, he no sooner entered my home when he charged my fifty gallon tropical fish tank and banged violently on the glass.

"What are those?" he shrieked as he pointed at the catfish. "What's the name of that plant? What's a fish's tail called?"

In all honesty, I seriously considered throwing this oversized angel fish in the tank. For my sister's sake, however, I decided to answer Brad's questions. After all, he was only trying to learn new words.

With all the enthusiasm I could muster, I patiently provided a name for each and every object in the tank about which he asked. In a way, I served as Brad's instructor, carefully teaching him the meaning of certain words, an example of the *didactic approach* to language instruction. However, Brad quickly became bored with my lessons and wandered off.

Terribly restless, Brad bounced over to the stereo system, my prized possession, and began fingering the speakers and tugging on the dials. Seeing this, I immediately grabbed his arm, pulled him from the stereo and shoved him in a chair.

"What's with this neurotic kid?" I bellowed at my wife. "This week is going to be complete insanity unless I control him."

Leaping out of his chair, Brad suddenly made a mad dash for the front door. I tackled him, and he began screaming at me.

"Leave me alone!" he howled. "I'm going home to tell my mommy you called me a bad name. I'm not neutonic—you are!" Why, this precocious brat had *inferred* from the tone of my voice and the other words in the sentence that neurotic was not a nice term. Though he may not have known the specific meaning of the word, he sensed quite accurately that it was no compliment. Unable to convince Brad that a neurotic is a "kind" person, I ended up apologizing to this six-year-old maniac. By the end of the week, both Brad and I were glad the visit was over.

Like Brad, each of us is constantly acquiring new words didactically and inferentially. For example, whenever we look up an unfamiliar term in the dictionary, ask a friend the meaning of a word, or weather a vocabulary lesson in English class, we are learning language didactically. In contrast, each time we figure out the meaning of a word without the help of dictionaries or people, relying, instead, on other terms in the sentence for guidance, our inferential ability is at work. Evidently, both approaches contribute much to our language development.

ARE MEANINGS IN PEOPLE OR WORDS?

If words are only sounds to which individuals associate a learned meaning, are meanings in people or words?

The answer to this riddle can be found in the following story which was scribbled on the dashboard of a 1956 Chevy.

It was a typical Friday night in Chicago for these five college students. Bored and restless, they engaged in the futile ritual of asking one another, "What do you want to do tonight?" As always, there were no exciting, new answers, only the same dull suggestions: playing poker, drinking beer, cruising through the neighborhood in search of females. Then Stu called.

He told them that several female telephone operators from rural sections of Illinois were staying at a nearby hotel. According to Stu, the women could be picked up easily, if the students payed them an unexpected visit at the hotel. Titillated by the thought of seducing strange rural females, the college students decided to take his advice.

After entering the hotel secretly, they used the back stairs to reach the floor on which the operators were living. Locating the correct room, Ray, the joker in the group, knocked on the door. With the appearance of an attractive young woman, Ray said he was taking a survey and would like to know if she was a "good girl or pragmatic girl?"

"Pragmatic!" she screamed. "Watch your dirty mouth. You're not going to use that language around here. I'm calling the manager."

Before the students could leave the establishment, hotel security nabbed the group and turned them over to the local police. Though they explained to the arresting officers that "pragmatic" was not an obscene term, the students were still charged with disorderly conduct.

CASE ANALYSIS. This communication breakdown is not a figment of my imagination; it did happen. Let's find out why it occurred.

Like all words, pragmatic is only a collection of sounds to which the distressed telephone operator associated a meaning. For some reason, however, our heroine imposed the wrong meaning on these sounds. In so doing, she incorrectly concluded that poor Ray was a pervert when, in truth, he was simply making a pass at her.

Certainly, the operator is not the first person who ever misunderstood a word. A common occurrence, language misunderstandings happen because words in themselves have no meaning; it is individuals who make them meaningful. That is, since words are merely sounds, they only become meaningful when a person attaches a meaning to them. And because no two people have had identical language training, individuals sometimes associate different meanings to the same word, certainly the case in the preceding scenario.

For example, as a college student, Ray had been exposed to a host of word meanings which he stored away for future use. In contrast, since our high school educated operator received modest language training, she could not identify as many words as Ray. In fact, when the operator heard the word pragmatic, an unfamiliar term, she guessed what it meant, an inference based primarily on the context of the sentence: "Are you a good girl or pragmatic girl?"

Had the operator's language training been similar to Ray's she would have imposed the correct meaning on pragmatic.

In answer to the riddle, then, meanings are in people not words. It couldn't be any other way, since words are only sounds.

Moving on, let's examine the different types of meanings we soak up throughout our lives. Consider connotative and denotative word meanings.

CONNOTATIVE AND DENOTATIVE MEANINGS

Can I level with you? I sure hope so because I have something very important to say. It's my pet cantaloupe; it just died. Once the pride and joy of Schwartz's fruit market, my loving, sensitive, beautiful cantaloupe has passed away. Certainly, death at any age is hard on the loved ones; however, it is particularly sad when the victim is only three days old—my cantaloupe's unlucky number.

Why, this fruit had so much to live for. Money, excitement, adventure, big melons, fast push carts; it could have had them all. But God stepped in and took my cherished sphere to that big fruit basket in the sky.

I'm lost without my cantaloupe. I think I'll get drunk and hussle a honeydew.

Were you moved by my words? Did you feel like sighing, crying, or laughing? If you're reasonably sane, you probably laughed. However, had the victim been a three-day-old child, my words would have disturbed you; let's find out why.

Terms like death, God, beautiful, sensitive, adventure, money, and excitement can stir emotions, arousing either positive or negative feelings. To some degree, most words have an emotionally stirring quality, otherwise referred to as an *affective* connotative meaning.

In addition, many of the words in "cantaloupe love" also have a personal meaning, commonly called an *informative* connotative meaning. As an example, though the dictionary defines death as the termination of life—the literal or *denotative* meaning of the word—many people have a more personal conception of death and dying. For some, death means that the body no longer lives but the spirit still survives. Others define death as the act of exchanging one's physical body with that of another being, as in the case of reincarnation. Like death, most terms have a personal meaning which often varies from individual to individual.

Accordingly, if the cantaloupe affair tugged at your heartstrings, it was because you considered terms like death, love, and God to have highly emotional connotative meanings. In contrast, those of you who were unaffected by my tale of woe probably found the language connotatively uninspiring; nevertheless, you still understood the passage, for you were familiar with each term's denotative meaning—the dictionary definition.

Returning to affective connotative meaning, let's take a closer look at this dimension of language.

Devil Terms

Broad-shouldered jocks shutter, and fear and terror sweep the classroom at the mention of the following: TEST, MIDTERM, FLUNKED, and the triple whammy COMPREHENSIVE FINAL EXAM. In fact, if a teacher wants to thin a crowded class he need only use the preceding terms the first day of instruction:

> "We will have four hundred *tests* this semester which most of you will *flunk* miserably. For the *comprehensive final exam,* you will be expected to know all scientific discoveries since 332 B.C."

What is it about these words that make strong men quake? Each has a negative affective connotation and is thus considered a devil term.

Devil terms jar the listener's emotional equilibrium; they enrage, offend, and incite people. In the 1950's, for example, the word communist headlined the devil term circuit; it shocked Americans, paralyzing them with fear. The social activism of the sixties intensified the negative connotations associated with some old devil terms like segregation, discrimination, genocide, and war. That period also produced some new devil words—escalation, pacification, search and destroy—each a by-product of the Vietnam War. More recently, terms such as unemployment, inflation, and busing stirred the emotions of the American public.

No doubt about it, devil words can alienate a speaker from an audience. On an interpersonal level, these terms can cause discord even violence. Consider.

Can you imagine turning off sixty women at the same time? I accomplished this Woody Allen feat the first time I spoke at a local chapter meeting of the National Organization of Women, the political arm of the female liberation movement. How did I do it? Well, I simply raised my hand during the question and answer period and naively queried, "Do you girls believe that the proposed equal rights amendment will help ladies achieve their social goals?"

No sooner did I finish when a young female jumped to her feet, glared in my direction, and then angrily accused me of being a "male chauvinist pig." "Chauvinist!" I cried, my liberal heart bleeding profusely. "What kind of remark is that? Not only is it untrue but it's rude as hell."

We exchanged insults until the chairperson restored order. I returned to my seat, baffled by the incident.

CASE ANALYSIS. Simply put, my choice of words caused the fracas. That is, in phrasing my initial question, I instinctively used "girl" and "lady," devil terms for many female liberationists. To a feminist, these words are offensive because they reduce adult females to little girls—helpless, naive, and immature. In fact, some liberationists believe that women will be denied real power as long as men perceive them as children.[1] No wonder the audience blanched when I asked my question.

Why was I upset with the vocal female? I resented being called a "male chauvinist pig," particularly since I considered myself a liberated individual. Angered by the woman's devil terms, I aggressively attacked her which only intensified hostilities. Emotionally aroused, neither of us could discuss the issue intelligently. It appears, then, that this hostile interpersonal conflict was caused by devil terms.

Though the feminist and I reacted negatively to each other's language, many people would have found our choice of words perfectly acceptable. For example, had the audience been composed of women with more traditional beliefs, girl and lady would not have elicited a hostile reaction. Similarly, if I did not fancy myself a liberated male, I might have laughed when called a chauvinist. In short, listeners' attitudes determine their emotional response to a word.

To accurately predict the impact of our language on listener behavior, it appears we ought to have some idea what the other person believes in. With this information, we can choose our words more intelligently, selecting terms that will turn on rather than turn off the listener.

Language Turn-Ons: God Terms

Unlike devil terms, god words excite the imagination, producing warm, positive feelings. Loaded with positive affective connotations, these terms can make us smile or laugh. Possessing almost a magical quality, god terms are powerful, capable of enthralling even the dullest listener.

In the past, words like God, America, freedom, and patriotism would raise goose bumps on any arm. Sensing this, politicians have been known to sprinkle each speech with a few of these words to stir an audience. Though the preceding terms can still excite individuals, it seems they have lost some of their intensity over the years.

Of course, there are the old standbys: love, mother, truth, justice, and equality—each word capable of evoking positive feelings in most people. Let's not forget the economic god terms of our era—status, power, and wealth.

On an interpersonal level, god terms can bring people closer together. In complimenting someone, for example, we often shower the person with god words: "You're a *beautiful* person." "What a *great* job." "I'm *proud* of you." Naturally, the recipients of the praise not only feel good about themselves but are quite favorably disposed to the speaker. In fact, individuals experiencing marital problems are often advised by a counselor to compliment their partners more often, an effective technique for improving a relationship.

Similarly, words like love and care can strengthen an intimate union. Remember how good you felt when your beloved tenderly said, "I love you?" Now recall the surge of emotion you experienced as she softly whispered, "I care about you." An intimate relationship cannot survive very long unless both parties are willing to use the language of love, the ultimate god terms.

Watch Your Mouth!

Are you convinced that words are very powerful? They can enthrall or enrage a listener, tighten a relationship or alienate the participants. In short, we should pay close attention to *what* we say, while also noting the *way* we say it, which brings us to another topic.

MONOPOLIZING THE CONVERSATION: EXPRESSING YOURSELF THE WRONG WAY

Meet Julie, Milwaukee's most active mouth. If you have nothing to do all day, ask her how she's been; Julie will certainly tell you. You'll learn about her kids, her husband, her health, her clothes, her teeth, her childhood, and her scars in an unending stream of words, uninterrupted by even a breath. Forget about expressing yourself; Julie won't hear of it. In fact, those who "converse" with her just nod politely and hope she'll pass out from lack of oxygen.

Don't people like Julie make you angry? If you could, wouldn't you like to tell Julie off; but what would you say? You'd probably first tell "sweet" Julie that she talks too much. That is, she (1) speaks too long, (2) uses too many words to express a thought, and (3) does not give others a chance to interact. In a word, Julie is a monopolizer.

For example, instead of speaking between three and fifty seconds, the average length of time most communicators hold onto the floor, Julie's contributions far exceed this time limit. And since Julie rarely signals either verbally or nonverbally that she is finished talking, the other person has no chance to speak.

Bombarded by a steady stream of words, deprived of their speaking turns, those who converse with a monopolizer often dislike their partner. These negative feelings are intensified by the monopolizer's frequent use of the pronouns I, my, and me—a manifestation of a self-centered attitude.

Unsurprisingly, a successful interpersonal encounter does not usually have a monopolizer; all individuals have the opportunity to participate. This way, each person can reveal thoughts and feelings.

It seems, then, that our choice of terms, length of time we speak, and number of words we use can dramatically affect an interpersonal encounter. Why are people so influenced by what we say and the way we say it? Read on for the answer.

LANGUAGE AND CULTURE

Words are revered in the United States. We use them in contracts to formalize business dealings; we consider a man's word his bond. Given our training, it is not surprising we pay close attention to what people say and the way they say it.

In other cultures, however, words are not as powerful as they are in the United States. According to Edward Hall, language varies in importance from culture to culture. To amplify this point, the following case is provided.

The Fender Bender

It was raining and I had lost my way. Feeling sure I was near my hotel, I foolishly stopped my car on a steep incline and pulled out my map of this Japanese city. As I searched feverishly through the complicated street guide, my car was rolling backwards ever so slowly. On hearing the wild honking of the car behind me, I jammed my brakes, barely touching the auto's front fender. Certain I had not damaged the other vehicle, I assumed the driver would be satisfied with an apology. I was dead wrong.

Gesturing wildly, the driver ranted at me in Japanese while pointing to a crease in the hood of his Toyota. Unable to speak Japanese, I explained in sign language that I could not have damaged his hood. After we bantered like blind men for several minutes, I realized my Japanese friend just wanted to fix an old dent at my expense.

Before long the police arrived. The driver immediately caught the officer's attention and explained in Japanese that I had mutilated his poor Corolla. After listening to the story, the policeman turned to me and asked in perfect English if I was an American. "I sure am," I responded enthusiastically, feeling certain my nationality would impress him.

"Do you live in Japan or are you just visiting?" he inquired.

"Visiting," I said, a bit annoyed by what I thought was an irrelevant question.

Anxious to tell the cop my side of the story, I blurted out that I did not and could not have damaged the other car. Then I carefully proved it to him or so I thought. To my amazement, the cop completely ignored my story and told me I was under arrest.

"Arrest!" I howled. "I have no time to spend in jail. I've got three more countries to see in the next five days." At that point, the policeman grabbed my arm, handcuffed me, and threw me in the paddy wagon. Unlike John Wayne, I bawled all the way to the police station.

CASE ANALYSIS. Why did the policeman ignore my carefully presented words? How come the officer automatically believed the other driver even though his tale was obviously untrue? To answer these questions, you have to be familiar with the role of language in Japanese culture.

First, words are not revered in Japan. To the Japanese, words are merely verbal expressions that may or may not be true. In fact, this society is not particularly concerned with *what* a person says; it is more interested in *who* the speaker is.

In the preceding case, for example, the policeman questioned us more about our nationalities and occupations than the accident. He probed our backgrounds to determine which one of us was a more credible source. Since the other driver was a respected and long-standing member of the community, the officer assumed that his description of the accident must be accurate, no matter how absurd it may have seemed. It appears that the policeman was more persuaded by *who* we were than *what* we said.

In *Beyond Culture,* Edward Hall argues that there are many societies like Japan where a person's educational and social background speaks for itself, where words and arguments are of minimal import.[2] To succeed in these societies, otherwise known as *high context cultures,* an individual has to attend a select university and know many respected people in the community.

In contrast, a *low context society,* such as the United States, Germany, and Sweden, places considerable importance on a person's words. This type of society is preoccupied with oral and written agreements; it couldn't do without them. Interestingly, language contracts are not often used in a high context culture, for an individual's reputation is sufficient guarantee that a service will be performed.

In retrospect, it appears I was a victim of circumstance. Reared in a low context culture (United States), I naturally thought my words would convince the policeman of my innocence. However, since the officer was a product of a high context society (Japan), he disregarded my language and focused on my background, certainly unimpressive by Japanese standards.

Evidently, culture determines the significance of what we say. In addition, it frequently chooses our words for us. Let me elaborate.

Verbal Taboos

Think about it: Are people really supposed to rest in a restroom? Do the words "making love" accurately describe what you and your girl-friend did last Saturday night? When mom caught you and Clarence "necking and petting," what did she actually see?

In each case, the term(s) poorly describes what is really going on; however, we dare not use more specific language in the presence of others. To be more explicit is crude, rude, and lewd, or so we've been taught by mommy and daddy—the culture's most effective teachers. As a result, we avoid using certain words in public, for we know they are taboo.

Simply put, verbal taboos are the unmentionables of our language, words "so unpleasant and so undesirable that we cannot say them even when they are needed."[3] Our parents made it perfectly clear to us which words were taboo through a slap in the face and/or swift kick in the pants. We learned our lessons well, as demonstrated by our nagging habit of substituting an acceptable phrase like "making love" for its more explicit, tabooed counterpart. Since the culture determines what terms we should and should not use, it actually chooses our words for us.

Every society has a long list of tabooed words. In the United States, terms dealing with sex and physiology head the list. Some argue that these types of words are offensive because historically the human body was considered "dirty," a source of humiliation and embarrassment. Similarly, others suggest that explicit sexual language evokes guilty, shameful feelings in the listener, a result of being raised in a puritanical society. In truth, no one knows for sure why these terms became taboo.

Although most people react negatively to forbidden words, these terms do have a redeeming quality: They let us blow off steam nonaggressively. That is, individuals frequently mutter a few hard core no-no's to release angry feelings instead of physically abusing their furniture and friends. Despite the therapeutic value of tabooed terms, it is wise not to use them in the presence of others; they can devastate an encounter.

WORDS: A CONCLUSION

Are you satisfied? I took it off; I took it all off, just as I had promised.

In disrobing a word, I seductively peeled off each of its garments. First we peeked at the meaning of terms, the outer apparel, and discovered that meanings are in people not words. Then we stripped words of their meaning and oogled the bare structure of language—sounds. Finally, we probed a word's intimate zone and found that language derives its power from the culture in which it is spoken.

Excited? Aroused? Why not scream a tabooed word; it may help.

SUMMARY

1. Words are symbols.

    Essentially a collection of sounds, each word stands for an object or concept. Symbols all, words make communication possible.

2. Language is learned in stages.

    As infants, our first attempt to speak was babbling, otherwise called lallation. At one year old, each of us was capable of imitating others, the basis for language learning. As we grew older, we continued acquiring language didactically and inferentially.

3. Meanings are in people not words.

    As demonstrated, words are only sounds to which individuals associate a learned meaning. Because no two people have had identical language training, individuals sometimes associate different meanings to the same word.

4. Most words have a denotative and connotative meaning.

    Denotative meaning is the dictionary definition of a term. In contrast, the connotative dimension of a word is the personal meaning it has for many people.

5. Language can significantly affect an interpersonal relationship.

    God terms evoke positive feelings in people while devil terms can devastate an encounter. In addition, those who use too many words, depriving others of their turn to speak, also alienate people.

6. Words derive their power from the culture in which they are spoken.

    Words vary in importance from culture to culture. For example, in a low context society like the United States, language is revered. In contrast, a high context culture considers a person's educational and social background of paramount concern; words and arguments are of little importance.

PRACTICE CASE STUDY

About to be interviewed for a teaching position, Sam Brown, a recent college graduate, waited nervously outside the principal's office.

"I've got to make myself distinctive," he thought, "or I'll never get the job. There must be a hundred people applying for this position."

Hearing the secretary call his name, Sam realized it was time for him to turn on the charm. "How do you do, sir," Sam said to the principal. "I'm delighted to be in your most impressive school."

"It's nice to meet you Sam," the principal responded. "Have a seat and tell me about yourself."

Adrenalin flowing, Sam described his background and philosophy of education. "I intend to be an innovative, enthusiastic teacher. Though I believe in discipline, I think students should have room to grow." Sensing success, Sam added, "As you can see, I don't want to be a run-of-the-mill teacher. At heart, I'm really a revolutionary."

No longer smiling, the principal abruptly ended the interview. Sam did not secure the position.

EXPLORATORY QUESTIONS

1. What god terms did Sam use to charm the principal?

2. Why do you think his language was initially successful?

3. Did Sam utilize a devil term? How did this affect the encounter?

4. Speculate on why the principal reacted so negatively to Sam's verbal transgression.

5. If the principal had been from a high context society, would he have reacted as he did to Sam's language? Explain.

ADDITIONAL PROJECTS

1. From what you know about a high context society, rewrite the preceding dialogue to reflect that culture's orientation toward language.

2. What advice could you offer Sam that might help him in future job interviews.

INTERPERSONAL COMMUNICATION EXERCISES

1. Is a word only sounds to which individuals associate a learned meaning? Let's find out.
   A. With a partner, develop a new language. To accomplish this, create words by associating objects and/or concepts to gibberish. Carefully note the new words you have constructed.

    B. After you have developed ten words, use the language. Teach someone else your language.

2. This exercise demonstrates that word meanings often vary from person to person.
    A. Divide the class into groups of four to six members. Each member should note in writing what the following terms mean:

        love
        racist
        stoned
        jive
        God
        communist
        freedom
        justice

    B. Group members should disclose their responses and discuss them. Why did individuals react so differently to the words?

3. Interested in verbal taboos? Let's discover why individuals use "dirty" words.
    A. Interview four people, two men and two women. The subjects should be about the same age. Ask each of them the following questions; prepare additional questions as well.
      1. When do you use obscene words most?
      2. Why do you use them at those times?
      3. What obscene words do you utilize most often?
      4. Do you ever use obscenities to release pent-up emotions?
    B. Analyze the responses, noting differences and similarities between and among sexes. Discuss your findings in class.

NOTES

[1] Robin Lakoff, "Language and Woman's Place," *Language and Society,* vol. 2 (1973), pp. 45–80.

[2] Edward Hall, *Beyond Culture* (New York: Doubleday, 1976).

[3] S. I. Hayakawa, *Language in Thought and Action* (New York: Harcourt Brace Jovanovich, 1941), p. 95.

CHAPTER **5**

Struttin' and Bumpin':
On Communicating Nonverbally

Dressed in a colorful shirt, gold double knit pants, and patent leather shoes, Don Dapper, the individual who arranged the gathering, marched brightly into the large room. Smiling broadly, Don scanned the setting before greeting the "guests."

Gathered are Don's friends and relatives, some of whom he has not seen in years. Sitting in the corner, head buried deep in her hands, is Mable Worth, Don's cousin. Uncle Hercus, normally the family clown, walks slowly across the room, head bowed and expressionless. On seeing Don, Hercus approaches him.

"Don, I'm so sorry. Your wife was such a good person," he whispers sympathetically.

Still smiling, Don accepts the condolence, chuckles to himself, then prances over to another mourner.

Though Don did not speak, he did convey his thoughts nonverbally. His gait, clothing, and facial expression may have communicated to you that he was the recipient of a large life insurance policy. You may have also concluded that Don was so overcome with grief he was acting irrationally.

On the other hand, it seemed that Uncle Hercus and Ms. Worth mourned the woman's passing given their posture, facial expression, and tone of voice. Found typically at funerals, their nonverbal behaviors communicate grief.

In short, actions speak as loudly as words. A fascinating and often misunderstood "language," nonverbal communication is explored in the following pages.

COMMUNICATING NONVERBALLY: BASIC DIMENSIONS

A never-ending process, we are constantly transmitting nonverbal messages through our body movements and appearance. Also included in the nonverbal domain, according to Ruesch and Kees, is the communication of artifacts found in the environment like art objects, architectural structures, even the display of material possessions.[1] Further, olfactory communication—the "messages" we receive through our nose—and the nonverbal aspects of speech—rate, pitch, volume, resonance, and hesitation—are frequently considered nonverbal terrain. In examining this broad topic, a wide range of nonverbal areas will be considered, including . . .

PINCHING, SQUEEZING, AND GRABBING: COMMUNICATING THROUGH TOUCH

She greeted me with a kiss and an embrace. While talking to me, she constantly touched my shoulder and hands. Upon leaving for the evening, she hugged me.

No, this individual was not my mother, wife, girlfriend, or lover. It was Susan, a grad student's wife with whom my spouse and I had just spent an evening. What's more, we had only known Susan for a few weeks.

In truth, Susan freely hugged, kissed, and touched me each time my wife and I socialized with her and her hubby. Unsurprisingly, whenever Susan displayed what appeared to be flirtatious behavior, I froze and my spouse began grinding her teeth, an indication that she was seriously considering tearing Susan's head off.

Don't get me wrong; I tried to discourage Susan's behavior. Like a boxer, I found myself bobbing and weaving to avoid her touch. As though playing musical chairs, I instinctively changed my seat whenever Susan was close enough to lay one on me.

Tired of this keystone cop existence, afraid my wife might one day commit involuntary woman slaughter, I suggested to her that we find new friends. Happily, I received no argument from my beloved.

CASE ANALYSIS. As demonstrated in the preceding scenario, touch is a form of communication. Holding, embracing, or just brushing another person can be interpreted as signs of affection, friendship, sexual intimacy, even hostility. In determining what a body contact means, we take into account the toucher's identity, the setting in which it occurred, and the part of the body touched.

In Susan's case, for example, my wife and I naturally assumed her "message" was of a sexual nature. Having known her for only a short time, Susan's behavior could not be easily dismissed as an act of friendship. Her frequent hugs and kisses also complicated matters for they are considered intimate body contacts. Besides, Susan was mandated by society to bestow these intimacies upon her husband, not me.

Since Susan touched the wrong person, at the wrong time, and in the wrong way, it is not surprising we thought she was interested in me. Though our evaluation seemed reasonable, we were wrong; Susan was only a "toucher," an often misunderstood individual in a society like ours.

Touching: American Style

America is basically a noncontact society, according to Edward Hall and others.[2] On the average, we touch one another publicly less than once during a three minute conversation. When we do connect, it is usually by brushing a person's arm; holding, kissing, and embracing are not frequently displayed.

In addition, touching is primarily reserved for an enduring relationship, be it husband/wife, parent/child, or the like. Though friends can occasionally touch one another, excessive physical contact often creates interpersonal problems, as demonstrated in the preceding case. Unable to freely express ourselves through body contact, Americans, according to Desmond Morris, turn to secondhand intimacies—a massage, a manicure, a physical examination—to satisfy their psychological desire to be touched.[3]

In this type of society, is it any wonder individuals like Susan are frequently criticized? Euphemistically called "touchers" or "physical people," these persons are often mistaken for dirty old men or sexually starved women; however, they are only expressing themselves nonverbally.

Touching Your Way to Happiness

Even in a noncontact culture like ours, touching plays a vital role in many types of encounters. As infants and children, we required frequent tactile stimulation from our parents. Deprived of physical contact—a sign of love and affection—the young child may be psychologically impaired. Moreover, studies have shown that a surprisingly large number of disruptive, even violent children were not fondled enough during infancy. To develop into a happy, well-adjusted adult, a child needs the warmth, tenderness, and security that only a touch can provide.

Our most intimate adult relationships are also greatly influenced by touching. Trained to be emotionally unexpressive, many males, for example, shy away from using a gentle touch or caress to communicate soft feelings to their partners. This often frustrates females who, according to Montagu, are encouraged as children and adults to express tender feelings through physical contact.[4] Unsurprisingly, tactile incompatibility upsets the male/female relationship particularly in matters of sexuality where touching is synonymous with intimacy. In fact, therapists like Masters and Johnson frequently treat sexual problems by teaching both partners how to satisfy each other's tactile needs.

In addition to enhancing the male/female encounter, touching can improve professional relationships as well. Medical researchers have found, for example, that patients respond favorably to the soft touch of nurses, doctors, and other health care personnel. Fearful and anxious, hospitalized patients frequently need to be physically reassured that someone empathizes with them. Similarly, a gentle touch, hold, or embrace from a therapist can help a client through an emotional crisis. What's more, in group therapy, the counselor often encourages the other participants to stroke a troubled member.

It seems, then, that touching influences the development of our psyches and our relationships. Though we need to be held, caressed, and embraced, only certain people are permitted close enough to stroke us intimately. Frequently considered territorial intruders, those who stand too close to us are admonished for their behavior. Wonder why?

TOO CLOSE FOR COMFORT: DISTANCE AND COMMUNICATION

As soon as the elevator door opens, an impatient hoard of people, including yourself, crowd into this tiny cubicle. With everyone jammed together, the lift slowly ascends, stopping suddenly between floors—an obvious mechanical failure. Surrounded by people, unable to move, how would you feel and behave?

Seemingly trapped in this dense crowd, your blood pressure would rise substantially, possibly resulting in head pains, dizziness, and double vision. Deprived of personal space, your emotional fuse would shorten, a prelude to hostile arguments with the others. You could not survive indefinitely in these close quarters, for the stress would be too much to bear.

You see, each of us requires a certain amount of space in which to live. Not only should a room be large enough to wander through freely, but there must be sufficient distance between the occupants. Without proper living space, individuals experience much stress, according to Edward Hall, noted expert on interpersonal distance. Unable to function effectively in this climate, a person's behavior and bodily functions are disrupted substantially.

Hans Seyle discovered, for example, that people are more aggressive, defensive, and violent in overcrowded situations.[5] Similarly, John Calhoun inferred from his experiments with rats that excessive crowding among humans can produce extreme social disorganization, including panic, murder, even cannibalism.[6] Indeed, our very survival depends on proper spacing, for the stress caused by overpopulation of the earth may eventually shorten our lives, speculates Konrad Lorenz, a German ethologist.[7]

Sensing the importance of personal space, each of us regulates our "territory" in certain ways. Consider.

Making Time with Distance: Space Speaks

It's Friday night and you are at a local tavern frequented by university students. While sipping a drink at the bar, you are approached by a young male.

Planting himself about three and a half feet from you, he strikes up a conversation. During the encounter, you notice he is moving closer to you. Now standing about one foot from your nose, his presence is overwhelming. What's your first thought?

Regardless of your gender, you would certainly wonder why this stranger had invaded your personal space, trespassed on your "turf." While slowly backpeddling to avoid his presence, you might interpret his behavior in one of several ways.

If you're a woman, for example, you might have concluded that the unfamiliar man was trying to seduce you. Standing within your intimate zone—marked by the tip of your nose to one and a half feet from your body—the stranger had invaded a territory normally reserved for lovers, boyfriends, and other intimates. Because such personal activities as lovemaking and comforting are usually conducted in this zone, the eager male was certainly not asking for directions.

On the other hand, a man might have interpreted the stranger's intrusion as a sign of homosexuality. Given the function of this zone, it is not surprising that male trespassers are often forcibly removed from intimate terrain.

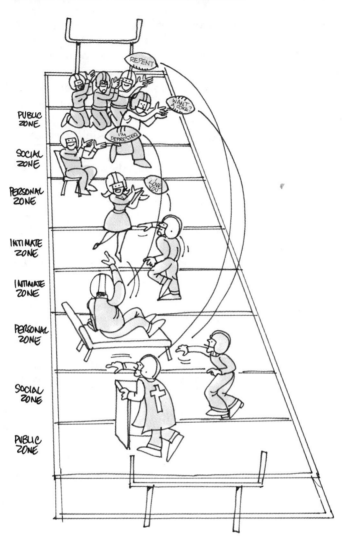

In addition to the intimate area, we have a personal, social, and public zone, each serving a different purpose. Surrounded by these zones, our spatial "territory," we are constantly interpreting the distance at which individuals converse; in short, space speaks.[8] Let's examine the remaining spatial zones.

PERSONAL ZONE. According to Edward Hall, the personal zone starts one and a half feet from the body and extends about four feet. In his study of proxemics—the way individuals regulate space—Hall found that people frequently disclose private thoughts and feelings in this zone; accordingly, only friends and relatives are permitted inside its borders. Moreover, we often assume that two people have an enduring relationship just because they communicate at personal distance. Writes Hall, "A wife can stay inside the circle of her husband's personal zone without impunity. For another woman to do so is an entirely different story."[9]

SOCIAL ZONE. Reserved for impersonal social conversation, this zone, beginning about four feet from the body, is where we conduct most of our daily interactions. A safe zone in which to converse, it signals to others that the communicators are engaged in superficial conversation.

Most formal encounters often transpire at the far phase of social distance, approximately five to twelve feet from the body. For example, business meetings are frequently conducted at this distance because office furniture is usually placed six to eight feet apart. Similarly, physicians and lawyers often interact from behind a large desk which spaces them at least seven feet from their clients. Those who converse at the far phase of the social zone appear detached, objective, and serious.

PUBLIC ZONE. Beyond twelve feet is the public zone. At this distance, speakers address audiences, and public figures formally greet supporters. Separated from the crowd, individuals who communicate at public distance are frequently viewed as special or important. As such, their message is often seriously considered.

Spatial Communication: Potential Hazards

As demonstrated, space speaks. In fact, individuals often misunderstand one another's spatial speech. For starters, reflect on the following case.

A member of a computer dating service, Chuck has been going out on blind excursions for months. Unsuccessful on his previous dates, Charles is hoping desperately that this time the computer will not fail him.

Arriving early for his date, he finds Juanita, his computer female, standing outside her home. While exchanging social niceties, Chuck notices that she is standing unusually far from him. Uncomfortable conversing at five feet, Charles tries to narrow the distance between them only to find Juanita backing up.

"Looks like another winner," he remarks to himself. "Does this one need a wedding ring before she can be a little friendly?"

Reluctantly, Charles escorts computer date number forty-two to his car. Once inside, Juanita plants herself firmly against the passenger door, arms wrapped tightly around her body.

"My God, she must think I'm an animal," Charlie concludes. "I'll get her to sit closer to me if it's the last thing I do."

As the car speeds down the street, Charles turns sharply at the first corner, throwing Juanita head first in his direction. Quickly regaining her balance, she finds Charlie's hand on her shoulder, blocking her return to the passenger door. As Juanita slowly moves away from him, Charles tries vainly to hold on to her shoulder. Loosing his grip, he watches her descend to the other side of the car.

"I've had it with this woman," decides Charlie. "I guess she just finds me repulsive."

CASE ANALYSIS. In addition to communicating verbally, our characters transmitted messages through the distance at which they interacted. Expecting Juanita to converse initially at about four feet, the close phase of the social zone, Chuck naturally thought her distant spatial selection indicated that she was not overjoyed with him. Similarly, Juanita probably found Chuck extraordinarily aggressive and disrespectful since in her country, Colombia, South America, men usually converse with women at about five feet, a morally appropriate distance for a Latino heterosexual encounter.[10] By misinterpreting each other's distance patterns, Chuck and Juanita destroyed a potential relationship.

The preceding case actually happened; in fact, it is just one of many misunderstandings that can occur when individuals are unfamiliar with one another's spatial preferences. As demonstrated, this type of breakdown is particularly evident in the cross-cultural encounter since the communicators often have different distance patterns, a topic thoroughly discussed in Chapter 9.

Like many nonverbal signals, spatial communication often goes unnoticed because it is right under our nose, which brings us to another area.

"I CAN SMELL A CROOK": OLFACTORY COMMUNICATION

Though I am not sure we can identify a thief by smell, it is true that odor communicates. One of the oldest forms of communication, odor plays a vital role in the lives of most animals. In helping wildlife to locate food, odor sustains life. What's more, many animals, including dogs and rats, rely on odor to identify their mate and determine whether he or she is sexually aroused. Finally, moths, bees, and other insects depend on smell to locate sustenance that may be a great distance away.

Unlike animals, human beings do not rely heavily on odor for information about the world. Once a highly developed sense, it seems that smell decreased in importance for humans when their evolutionary ancestors left the ground and took to the trees where good vision was needed to survive. Hence, our sense of smell ceased developing when we became arboreal beings, according to many zoologists.

Despite its evolutionary decline, smell is still a viable communicator for *Homo sapiens*. Consider.

The Language of Odor

Escorted into a laboratory, you find yourself in front of two small boxes, each with a hole on top from which a smell emanates. At the direction of the investigator, you place your nose by each hole, deeply breathing in the odor. After the experiment, you are asked to identify the gender to which each odor belongs. Could you do it?

You certainly could, according to Michael Russell, the University of California primate researcher who conducted the preceding experiment.[11] In fact, he found that ninety-five percent of those who sniffed the unseen apparel of an unknown wearer could correctly identify the individual's gender. In describing the odors, the subjects remarked that the male scent was musky and the female scent was sweet, though none of the wearers had used soap, perfume, or deodorant for twenty-four hours prior to the experiment. It seems, then, that our nose can distinguish between men and women, certainly a rudimentary form of olfactory communication.

In addition to gender discrimination, it appears we can also identify certain people by their odor. For example, Charles Darwin noted in the nineteenth century that infants recognized their mother's scent. His observation was confirmed by a series of recent experiments which found that infants as young as six weeks old are aroused by their mother's odor and unaffected by that of other women.

In certain cultures, odor is also used to distinguish between friend and foe. For example, to appear honest and sincere in Arabic societies, communicators must share their breath with others. Those who refuse to breathe into another person's face are considered suspicious and untrustworthy. In contrast, Americans are trained to keep their breath to themselves. No wonder Arabs and Americans frequently misunderstand each other's olfactory signals.

A relatively unexplored area of communication, olfaction may be more vital to human interaction than we ever thought. Researchers may find that odor is just as communicative as gesture, posture, and facial expression, the body movements examined in the following section.

BODY LANGUAGE

Remember the time you suspected your beloved had cheated on you? As he spoke, you watched his face and hands closely as though they told the real story. After he finished protesting his loyalty, you walloped him because his face was the picture of infidelity.

Whenever we converse with others, we are telling two stories—one with words, the other with our body. Though sometimes difficult to understand, the tale being spun by our gestures, facial expressions, and posture is just as meaningful as verbal description, according to Ray Birdwhistell who developed kinesics, the study of body movements. Birdwhistell argues that the body has a language all its own, a language we *learn* at an early age.

Learnin' Body Talk: The Culture Made Me Do It

While each of us is born with the capacity to communicate nonverbally, it seems that the culture selects our body movements for us. As children, we learn the appropriate postures, gestures, and

facial expressions and are also taught what many of them mean. Like verbal communication, our body language is acquired through cultural conditioning. To illustrate this, let's take a closer look at posture and gesture.

Waiting outside a professor's office, you attempt to strike up a conversation with another student. As usual, you introduce yourself, expecting a similar introduction from your partner. Instead, the student suddenly throws himself to the ground, crawling and squirming on all fours directly in front of you. After only a few seconds on the floor, he returns to his seat and humbly introduces himself to you. On hearing the professor's voice, the student loudly snaps his fingers, excuses himself, and departs.

Certainly, you would have concluded that the crawling student had experienced either an epileptic seizure or a nervous breakdown. You might have also been confused and perturbed when he snapped his fingers at you, for no waiter was in sight. Though your reactions were only natural, there was really no reason to be uptight.

You see, the student with whom you were conversing was from Dahomey, a West African country on the Northern coast of the gulf of Guinea. Trained to use certain postures and gestures, the student was neither sick nor mentally disordered. In his culture, crawling on the floor is an act of humility not a sign of emotional disturbance. Similarly, snapping one's fingers—an impolite gesture in the United States—merely signals in Dahomey that a communicator must depart. Unfamiliar with this culture, you could have easily misinterpreted the student's behavior.

If Gordon Hewes' research is accurate, you might experience similar difficulties in other societies.[12] He found, for example, that the inhabitants of many cultures sit and stand quite differently; in fact, so differently, that an unsuspecting American would not know what was going on. Similarly, many of the gestures you might perceive throughout the world would also be quite confusing.

Like posture, the type of gesture displayed and its meaning are largely determined by the culture. For instance, in noting that Eastern European Jews gesture more frequently and less expansively than Southern Italians, David Efron, an anthropologist, demonstrated that cultures train their inhabitants to gesture in certain ways.[13] This was confirmed by Ray Birdwhistell who discovered that many societies use different gestures to communicate the same concept. As an illustration, when an Italian man pulls his right ear lobe with his right forefinger and thumb, he is signaling that a pretty woman is passing by. An Arab male, however, will stroke his beard to convey the identical message.

To understand many postures and gestures, it appears we have to be acquainted with the communicator's culture. Once this is accomplished, we can more accurately determine the meaning of these body movements. Take Americans, for example.

He Loves Me, He Loves Me Not: Postures and Gestures in America

Strongly attracted to him, you watch his every move to see whether the feeling is mutual. Peering at his herculean form, you notice that (1) he leans forward instead of back whenever he converses with you from a seated position; (2) he always faces you directly when communicating; (3) and upon leaving, he uses an expansive hand gesture that seems to reach out for you. Does he care? He may, according to Albert Mehrabian.

After conducting extensive research on nonverbal communication, Mehrabian found that Americans convey both positive and negative feelings through posture and gesture.[14] He discovered, for example, that when a communicator is attracted to someone the individual will lean forward in the chair and face the partner while speaking. Similarly, in departing, this communicator will frequently reach out for the other person, a gestural indication of interpersonal attraction.

Posture and gesture convey other feelings as well. Julius Fast argues that individuals who converse from a closed position—arms wrapped tightly around themselves, seemingly hiding their body from view—are communicating that they feel threatened and insecure.[15] Conversely, a high level of gesture activity coupled with an open, inviting posture is a sign of warmth and happiness, according to Dittman and Sarnesbury.[16] Finally, those experiencing an emotional depression normally gesture infrequently, while frustrated communicators frequently dangle their arms between their legs.

In addition to reflecting a person's emotional state, gesture and posture also transmit other messages. Consider.

JUST A LITTLE RESPECT. Slouching deep in his chair, arms dangling, legs straight out, Mark, a first grader, is about to be reprimanded for positioning his body this way.

"Sit up young man," she bellows loudly. "Sit up and pay attention if you know what's good for you."

Sound familiar? Like Mark, each of you probably received the same type of warning numerous times from teachers, parents, and other authority figures. Reminded constantly to "straighten up," you finally began standing erect in the presence of those you were supposed to respect. In so doing, you learned how to communicate attention and respect through posture.

Unsurprisingly, researchers have found that a person's posture is more informal and relaxed when communicating with someone of low status. No longer required to be perfectly erect, an individual's head and shoulders can droop substantially, a sign of equality, comfort, and rapport.

Finally, postures of respect and informality can be classified as nonverbal emblems, for they communicate the same message to most individuals in American society. In addition to certain postures, there are many hand gestures that can also be characterized as emblems, including the peace signal, the O.K. sign, and the infamous "finger." Learned early in life, these nonverbal expressions are rarely misunderstood.

Capable of transmitting a host of messages, posture and gesture have been extensively researched. Similarly, investigators have thoroughly examined facial expressions, our next nonverbal consideration.

Face to Face

Having just ordered a very expensive meal at an exclusive restaurant, you are eagerly waiting for the waiter to serve the special house soup. Supposedly a gustatory delight, this liquid delicacy is carefully placed on your table. Spoon in hand, you plunge the utensil into the cloudy water at which point a defunct, but large, black horsefly surfaces. Surprised and angered, you call the waiter over who smiles broadly while you complain. In fact, as your bellowing intensifies, his smiling increases, culminating in a soft but distinct giggle.

Certainly, you would have been enraged by the waiter's facial expression. Expecting a serious, concerned reaction, you instead received what appeared to be a happy response. However, before reporting this incident to his boss, you should realize a couple of things.

First, the waiter was Japanese. In Japan, interpersonal confrontations are avoided like the plague; harmony and cooperation are expected in all transactions. To engage in conflict is so embarrassing to native Japanese that they frequently smile and giggle when confronted. A sign of embarrassment, not joy, the waiter's facial expression would have been misinterpreted if you were unfamiliar with Japanese culture.

Having read this case, it should come as no surprise that certain facial expressions mean different things in different societies. For instance, the smile is not always an expression of happiness. Writes Birdwhistell,

> "A smile in one society portrays friendliness, in another embarrassment, and in still another may contain a warning that unless tension is reduced, hostility and attack will follow."[17]

Similarly, a surprised look in American society would be interpreted quite differently in Guam where raised eyebrows and widened eyes mean "leave me alone." In fact, Birdwhistell has identified so many cultural differences in nonverbal behavior that he claims there are no facial expressions, gestures, or postures that "provoke identical responses the world over."[18]

Unlike Birdwhistell, some researchers believe that facial expressions do not differ from culture to culture. For example, Paul Ekman found that each of the basic emotions—sadness, happiness, anger, frustration, and disgust—are expressed similarly in many societies.[19] His research partially confirmed Charles Darwin's early presumption that facial expressions are the same throughout the world.

It seems, then, that certain facial expressions may have the same meaning in many cultures. In contrast, the work of Birdwhistell, Mead, and others clearly indicates that each society has its own unique facial responses that may not be understood by outsiders. In truth, both findings are significant, for they suggest that facial messages may be difficult to understand and should be evaluated cautiously.

THE LANGUAGE OF LANGUAGE: PARALINGUISTICS

Strongly desiring to date someone new, you reluctantly ask a girlfriend to fix you up. Assured by her that the new male in your life is a "nice guy with a good personality"—a tipoff that he is nothing to look at—you seriously doubt whether you'll accept the date. With the ring of the telephone, you realize a decision must be made.

"Can I, um, talk to, um, Mary Doe?" the speaker haltingly inquires.

"Why this is she; who's calling?"

"Um, this is, um, Mark Doud. Your, um, girlfriend gave me your number," the caller mumbles in a nasal, high-pitched voice. "Um, did she tell you I was, um, going to call?"

"She sure did," you respond with vengeance in your heart.

After an extended silence, the caller asks hesitantly whether you would like to go out with him Saturday night. Would you accept?

Though I'm sure each female reading this scenario is kind and considerate, it would not surprise me if you passed up this date for two reasons. First, the caller's paralinguistic cues—pitch, rate, tone, and pause—may have created a most unfavorable impression. His nasal, high-pitched voice and frequent use of "um" might have convinced you that the caller was tense and insecure. Unable to see him, the caller's vocal cues would certainly not ease your mind about his appearance, the second reason for not accepting the date.

Evidently, *how* we speak is just as meaningful as what we say. Commonly called paralinguistics, the "how" includes a range of vocal cues which Trager places in four categories: (1) voice qualities—

pitch, range, rhythm, and resonance; (2) vocal characterizers—laughing, crying, snoring, coughing, clearing the throat; (3) vocal qualifiers—intensity (loud, soft), extent (drawl); (4) vocal segregates—hesitation (um, uh-huh) and silent pauses.[20]

You would be simply amazed at how communicative these vocal cues can be. Consider.

What a Voice!

If the male in the preceding case had a deep, throaty voice you probably would have accepted his invitation. According to Donald Addington's research, males who have this type of voice are perceived as masculine, realistic, mature, and well-adjusted.[21] In contrast, he found that men with a nasal, high-pitched voice are frequently stereotyped as effeminate, flighty, childlike, and testy. Though it seems absurd to judge a speaker's personality by vocal cues we do it every day.

A trademark of many female sex symbols, a breathy voice is associated with sensuality, beauty, and superficiality. Addington also discovered that women who have a throaty quality are frequently judged as unintelligent, masculine, lazy, boorish, unemotional, sickly, careless, even ugly! It seems we associate personality traits with every imaginable vocal cue, according to paralinguistic investigators.

Though voice alone does not accurately reflect an individual's personality, it can communicate a person's emotional state. As listeners, we can quickly identify an angry, happy, or impatient tone of voice. Similarly, we respond sympathetically to a sad voice. Apart from the words, it is vocal cues—particularly pitch, rate, inflection, and rhythm—which communicate a speaker's feeling to us.

For example, Davitz found that sadness is usually conveyed when a person uses a soft, low voice, pauses irregularly, and slurs enunciation.[22] Conversely, a happy voice transmits information more rapidly and is louder and higher than one of gloom. In short, Davitz argues that most human emotions can be communicated paralinguistically.

Finally, a word about "er," "ah," "um," and other speech hesitations. Frequently construed as signs of nervousness, these interjections take their toll on a speaker's image. If an individual uses too many "ers," they can damage credibility making the speaker less persuasive.

On Receiving Two Messages:
A Final Note on Paralinguistics

"I love you," he mumbled dispassionately. "Will you marry me?" he queried coldly. "I am sorry about your mother's death," she proclaimed happily.

Would you believe any of these statements? Probably not, for the speakers' words were contradicted by their paralinguistic cues. Having received two opposing messages—one linguistic, the other paralinguistic—you would seriously question the speakers' credibility.

In truth, each time we speak we transmit two messages, one through words, the other through paralinguistic cues. Sometimes these messages are at odds—"I love you," he said dispassionately—while, on other occasions, they are identical—"I am sorry about your mother's death," she remarked sympathetically. Sensitive to both messages, we often determine the speaker's truthfulness by comparing "what" the person said with "how" it was said.

Evidently, an individual's spoken words and paralinguistic cues are rich sources of information. We should pay close attention to both messages.

THE CLOSE OUT

Like a store owner closing out merchandise, I feel as though my major nonverbal inventory—touching, olfaction, body movements, distance, and paralinguistics—has been offered to the public. Having carefully examined the items on display, you should better understand why actions speak as loudly as words.

SUMMARY

1. Broadly defined, the nonverbal domain includes every aspect of our behavior, save the spoken word.

   We communicate nonverbally through touch, gesture, posture, olfaction, facial expression, eye contact, and other bodily expressions. Also considered nonverbal stimuli are distance, time, appearance, vocal sounds, and artifacts found in the environment.

2. An often misunderstood vehicle of communication, touch can either enhance or stifle a relationship.

   In relationships of intimacy, be they parent/child, husband/wife, or the like, touch is a necessary and meaningful form of communication. Outside these encounters, excessive touching can result in misunderstandings, for our society is basically non-contact oriented.

3. The distance at which individuals interact is as communicative as the words they use.

   Each time we penetrate a person's spatial zone, whether public, social, personal, or intimate, we convey a message. Apparently, space speaks.

4. A frequently neglected form of communication, smelling, commonly called olfactory interaction, is another way we receive information.

Relying primarily on odor, certain individuals can distinguish between genders, identify their parents, and determine whether a person is a friend or foe. It appears that odor may be more communicative than we ever thought.

5. Interpersonal messages are transmitted through gestures, posture, and facial expression.

Gesture, posture, and facial expression frequently differ from culture to culture. To understand what many of these bodily movements mean, it is often necessary to be familiar with the communicator's culture.

6. Be it pitch, rate, tone, or the like, an individual's paralinguistic cues communicate information to others.

Certainly, how we speak is just as meaningful as what we say. In fact, on the basis of vocal cues, we often evaluate a speaker's personality and emotional state.

PRACTICE CASE STUDY

Born and raised in Egypt, Dr. Habish is presently a professor of biology at a university in Chicago. Although he is now familiar with American customs, his first year in this country was a traumatic one; in fact, he almost lost his position at the university. Let's examine the sequence of events that nearly resulted in his dismissal.

His problems began the first day of biology class. Responsible for teaching the students how to use a microscope, Dr. Habish had them experiment with the device. While they examined several slides, he circulated through the room, closely watching each student manipulate the mechanism.

Upon approaching a busy learner that day, Habish leaned over the sitting student, placing his face about six inches from the learner's head. What's more, he frequently rested his arm on the student's neck or shoulder during the visit. Surprised by the professor's unusual behavior, several students speculated after class that Habish was a "dirty old man."

As the semester progressed, more and more students concluded that Habish was bisexual simply because he interacted so closely and often touched members of both sexes. Uncomfortable in his class, several students finally complained to the department chairman that the professor was on the make. Concerned about the allegation, the chairman informally asked several students about Habish's behavior. All agreed that he was certainly strange.

Outraged by the students' remarks, the chairman seriously considered dismissing Habish. If the university's communication specialist had not heard about the case, the professor would have been dismissed.

EXPLORATORY QUESTIONS

1. Why do you think Habish communicated so closely to his American students?

2. What conclusions could you draw from this case about American and Arabic distance patterns?

3. Why do you think Habish touched his students so frequently?

4. Would you say Arabs are a contact or noncontact people?

5. Why did Habish's students interpret his nonverbal behavior as a sign of bisexuality?

6. How do you think Habish might have interpreted his students' distance and contact behavior?

7. Could you speculate on how the communication specialist saved Habish's job?

ADDITIONAL PROJECTS

1. If you were the university's communication specialist, what type of educational program would you develop to avert similar crises in the future?

INTERPERSONAL COMMUNICATION EXERCISES

1. Distance Exercise
   Each of us behaves differently in a crowded situation. To determine how you would feel if your available space was suddenly reduced, participate in the following exercise.
   A. The class should be divided into groups of four to six members. Each group should make a circle and place one member in the middle. The remaining group members should walk towards the person in the center, cutting off the available space. Repeat this procedure with each group member.
   B. To vary this exercise, have each member enter the circle for a second time with eyes closed. The remaining members should invade the spatial zones of the person in the center until the individual signals them to stop. At this point, the

encircled communicator should try to estimate how close each group member is standing from the center.

2. Black Bag Exercise: Tactile Communication
   This exercise should help you determine just how much information can be received through touch.
   A. Bring a large paper bag to class filled with items of varying shapes, textures, and weights. Each class member should walk to the front of the room, place one hand in the bag, and attempt to identify the items through touch alone.
   B. In varying this exercise, have only one class member identify the items. After completing this, the individual should attempt to communicate the discoveries to the class nonverbally.

3. Paralinguistic Exercise
   Can you communicate an emotion simply through tone of voice? To discover how sensitive you are to vocalic cues, try this exercise.
   A. Pair off with a class member. Using only gibberish, transmit the following emotions to your partner: sadness, happiness, anger, sarcasm, love, sympathy, excitement, frustration, and boredom.
   B. After both of you have completed the exercise, discuss the difficulties you had transmitting and receiving each emotion.

NOTES

[1] Jurgen Ruesch and Weldon Kees, *Nonverbal Communication: Notes on the Visual Perspective of Human Relations* (Berkeley and Los Angeles: University of California Press, 1956).

[2] Edward Hall, *The Hidden Dimension* (New York: Doubleday, 1966).

[3] Desmond Morris, *Intimate Behavior* (New York: Random House, 1971).

[4] Ashley Montagu, *Touching: The Significance of the Skin* (Columbia University Press, 1971).

[5] Hans Seyle, *The Stress of Life* (New York: McGraw-Hill, 1956).

[6] John Calhoun, "Population Density and Social Pathology," *Scientific American*, vol. 206 (1962), pp. 139–146.

[7] Konrad Lorenz, *Man Meets Dog* (Cambridge: Riverside Press, 1955).

[8] Edward Hall, *The Hidden Dimension* (New York: Doubleday, 1966).

[9] Ibid., p. 120.

[10] Robert Shuter, "Proxemics and Tactility in Latin America," *Journal of Communication*, Summer, 1976.

[11] Michael Russell, *New York Times*, April 17, 1976.

[12] Gordon Hewes, "The Anthropology of Posture," *Scientific American*, (1957), pp. 123–132.

[13] David Efron, *Gesture and Environment* (New York: King's Crown Press, 1941).

[14] Albert Mehrabian, "Significance of Posture and Position in the Cum-

munication of Attitude and Status Relationships," *Psychological Bulletin*, vol. 71 (1969), pp. 359–372.

[15] Julius Fast, *Body Language* (New York, Lippincott, 1970).

[16] Arthur Dittman, "The Relationship Between Body Movements and Moods in Interviews," *Journal of Consulting Psychology*, vol. 26 (1962), pp. 480–487; Paul Sarnesbury, "Gestural Movement During Psychiatric Interviews," *Psychosomatic Medicine*, vol. 17 (1955), pp. 458–469.

[17] Ray Birdwhistell, *Kinesics and Context* (University of Pennsylvania Press, 1970), p. 34.

[18] Ibid., p. 34.

[19] Paul Ekman, "Constants Across Cultures in the Face and Emotion," *Journal of Personality and Social Psychology*, vol. 17 (1971), pp. 124–129.

[20] George Trager, "Paralanguage: A First Approximation," *Studies in Linguistics*, vol. 13 (1958), pp. 1–12.

[21] Donald Addington, "The Relationship of Selected Vocal Characteristics to Personality Perception," *Speech Monographs*, vol. 35 (1968), pp. 492–503.

[22] John Davitz, *The Communication of Emotional Meaning* (New York: McGraw-Hill, 1964).

CHAPTER 6

What's *Your* Game?
Exploring Interpersonal Manipulation

Rising at 6:00 A.M. on a Monday morning was a bit unusual for Phillip, a second grader. Rapidly pouring himself out of bed, he staggered noisily through the hall to the toilet which was adjacent to his parents' bedroom. After slamming the bathroom door, Phillip listened intently to discover whether he had disturbed his sleeping parents.

Detecting parental whispers, Phillip quickly plunged his index finger down his throat, causing him to gag and wretch loudly. For several minutes, strained grunts and groans exploded in the early morning darkness until Phillip's mother appeared at the bathroom door.

"What's wrong, Phillie?" she tenderly inquired.

Slowly opening the door, angelic Phillip, seemingly drained by his bout with nausea, whimpered, "I don't feel good, mamma. My stomach hurts; my head aches; I have pains all over."

After gently stroking Phillie's forehead, sympathetic mamma returned him to his room and tucked him in bed. There would be no school today for this little con man.

Though Phillip was only seven, he was an expert manipulator. Like most children, Phillie learned at an early age that fabrication, concealment, and fakery are convincing persuaders, particularly when one wants to stay home from school, be excused from the dinner table, or obtain a new bicycle. Strange as it may seem, little

Phillie sensed at age seven that authenticity and honesty often get in the way of achieving goals. Our tiny star was fully capable of controlling the thoughts and actions of children and adults, otherwise referred to as interpersonal manipulation.

We are all little Phillies, strategically altering our language and behavior to secure a variety of payoffs: a good job, a sought after date, some praise from a respected teacher, even a little attention from a busy girlfriend. Camouflaging our real thoughts and feelings with desirable facades, we frequently manipulate others without their knowledge. Consider.

THIS IS YOUR LIFE: REFLECTIONS ON IMPRESSION MANAGEMENT

This is your life, Mr. and Ms. Manipulator. In the next few pages, we will examine a variety of personal "images" you utilized during your glorious career as an interpersonal con man. Those who contributed most to the development of your manipulative façades—teachers, parents, and peers—have agreed to appear in the following pages. And now on with the analysis.

Recognize this person?

> "Though we didn't have much money, you were dressed better than any baby on the block. Wearing a cashmere diaper, Pierre Cardin baby sweater, and patent leather baby shoes, you were the epitome of style. From your appearance, no one would have ever guessed your father was unemployed."

That's right; it's your mother, Louise Image. It was her and your father who first introduced you to impression management, the art of constructing the most favorable public image, according to Erving Goffman. Your parents realized that apparel helps establish a person's image and thus selected baby garb that communicated your family was one of substance and style. Unaware at this time that your image was being "managed," you soon learned what impression management was all about.

> "At the tender age of two, your father and I began training you to dress, speak, behave, and sit properly while in the presence of others. This instruction continued until we felt people would be convinced that you were obedient, courteous, intelligent, and sociable; though at home, you were just another brat. In fact, if you embarrassed us in public, you heard about it."

Remember this period of your life, Mr. and Ms. Manipulator? No doubt about it, you received intensive training in impression management from your parents during early childhood. Orders—mom and dad constantly gave you orders: "Kiss grandma hello when

you see her." "Don't fight with your sister when you're around people." "Leave your sport coat on in the restaurant." "Always say
please and thank you in public." "Don't eat with your hands." "Wait
your turn." Having internalized these and other parental pronounce-
ments, you tried to control your actions and speech in public to
convey the most favorable impression. Why, you even selected the
appropriate garb for Mary Lou's birthday party, an indication that
you intuitively sensed the value of impression management at five
years old.

As you matured, you developed a host of public façades which
you shrewdly displayed at the appropriate time. An adroit manipulator now, you could disguise your real feelings with an appealing
exterior in order to elicit a favorable response from others. You
became a full-fledged player of what Goffman calls the expression
game, a contest waged by two or more individuals who have learned
the art of impression management.[1] To tell us more about your

involvement in expression games is someone who used to arouse the animal in you.

> "I remember when we first met; I thought you were so cool! There you were casually leaning against the bar, dressed in knickers, bobby socks, and a fedora. Ya know, I almost slid off my chair when I heard you grunt, 'Hey kosher, let's get it on, huh? huh?' I thought it was the coolest expression I had ever heard. But I knew you said it to everyone you seduced."

You'll never forget her, Mr. Manipulator. It's your childhood sweetheart, Henrietta McKinley.

Do you remember the evening Henrietta is describing? That night you carefully selected your attire, opening line, even your pose. Each was chosen to establish a cool, hip image, a marketable impression in the world of hussling. Henrietta was the first person with whom you successfully played the seduction expression game. To learn more about this game, let's find out what Albert Scheflen, a noted communication researcher, has discovered about courtship behavior.[2]

Scheflen found that individuals involved in courtship project a desirable image by altering a suprisingly wide variety of their nonverbal behaviors. Readying themselves for the encounter, the interactants lessen their slouch, decrease their belly sag, and straighten hunched shoulders. This is followed by the preening stage during which each individual rearranges hair and clothes to present the most provocative appearance. Finally, to make themselves more alluring, individuals attempt to pose and move seductively, which Scheflen calls actions of appeal and invitation. Included in this category are such behaviors as the cool posture, rolling of the pelvis, and protruding of the upper torso.

So you see, Mr. and Ms. Manipulator, your life has been a series of manipulative encounters during which you attempted to establish and preserve a personal image. Though I could find additional examples of impression management in your past—the interview, a business transaction, the first meeting with your in-laws—I think by now you understand the principle. I need not impress you any longer.

Admittedly, impression management is a small part of your life story as an interpersonal manipulator. You engage daily in a host of strategic games that entail far more than image building.

INTERPERSONAL GAMES: WHAT ARE THEY?

We are all salesmen covertly maneuvering others for our own personal gain. Though we should be honest and direct with one another, we frequently employ a series of strategic moves to secure an undisclosed "payoff" or goal. Commonly called game playing, this type of maneuvering is widespread in American culture.

Interpersonal games can be divided into two major categories: con games and head games. In a con game, a player's desired outcome or payoff is tangible—a sale, a lower price, a date, a satisfied customer. Head games, however, are played for psychological payoffs—reassurance, self-castigation, vindication—and are thus more intricate than con games. To illustrate the characteristics of both head and con games, the following sections examine several interpersonal games in each category.

CON GAMES

The con game is certainly no stranger to Americans. In a society like ours where individuals must compete daily for every imaginable item—a grade, a job, a book contract—is it any wonder we frequently manipulate one another? We have no choice, for to survive in the marketplace, be it economic, educational, or industrial, we must outmaneuver our competitors. For starters, let's take a look at a few interpersonal con games.

Polishing the Apple: The Grade Game

Many successful students will tell you that there is more to securing an excellent grade than doing well on a series of tests. In addition to possessing effective study habits, the proud holder of a B+ or better grade point average is sometimes an expert manipulator, capable of conning his teachers without them being aware of it. Utilizing a variety of strategies to achieve the payoff—a superior grade—the student gamester is a sight to behold. Consider the following case.

Marvin was not your typical student; he was a well-trained strategist who could manipulate just about any professor at will. I met this con man during my first semester at Marquette University and was immediately taken in by his act.

Marvin unfolded his game plan on the first day of class. Sitting in the front row, the master manipulator smiled pleasantly at me, nodding agreeably while I explained the course to the class. As though hanging on my every word, Marvin never took his eyes off me. He just reeked of seriousness, involvement, and concern; a trio that would snare any professor.

Marvin's manipulative web was not completely spun until he spoke with me privately after the initial class session. During the brief conversation, he praised my course, and also remarked enthusiastically that his scholarly interest seemed to parallel mine. After asking permission to visit me periodically to discuss our "mutual" concerns, Marvin politely terminated the discussion.

In the ensuing class periods, Mr. Manipulator really turned on the charm. He actively answered questions, continued to nod and smile while I lectured, and frequently contributed information that supported my position. For his efforts, Marv was rewarded at the end of the semester with a superior grade. No doubt about it, I was conned.

While Marv's game plan was more sophisticated than most, his manipulative strategies were not uncommon. In fact, you may have employed a few yourself, particularly in those difficult courses about which you were warned. Like Marv, on those occasions you probably experimented with one or more of the following maneuvers: strategic support, identification, and ingratiation. Let's first examine strategic support.

As indicated in an earlier chapter, each of us desperately wants to be accepted by others. To that end, we search peoples' language and facial expressions for positive feedback, a sign that our communication is appropriate and meaningful. Driven by our insatiable need for support, we are prey for individuals like Marv who dish out counterfeit approval to secure a desired payoff. Sensing that professors need to be stroked as much as any other human being, Mr. Manipulator was the epitome of support in the classroom.

For example, Marv's nod of agreement, fixed look, and mask of involvement made it patently clear that he thought my ideas were terribly significant. Similarly, Marv verbally supported me during visits to my office and through class contributions. He measured his every word and action in order to present the most supportive personal image.

Interestingly, the limited research conducted on strategic support in the classroom indicates that Marv's success was no accident. In one study, for example, a group of high school low achievers were trained in the art of strategic support.[3] After acquiring this skill, the students were told to bestow large doses of approval upon their unsuspecting teachers. The game plan paid off, for the investigators found after only a few weeks that the students not only received better grades, but the teachers treated them with greater respect and understanding.

"I'm Proud as Punch to Be Here": Identification and Ingratiation in the Classroom

Marv also sensed that people with similar attitudes and interests are attracted to each other; accordingly, he communicated early in the semester that his intellectual concerns paralleled mine. No matter what I was interested in, Marv intimated that he had been deeply concerned about the topic as far back as he could remember. Within a few weeks, Marv was able to demonstrate quite convincingly that he shared my enthusiasm about certain ideas and projects—a conspicuous display of identification.

Finally, Marv was an ingratiator; in fact, he could charm his way to an A. Always extraordinarily pleasant to his prey, Marv was the picture of innocence. No one would have believed that this bouncy, beaming, jovial young man—terribly well mannered and so very kind—was actually ingratiating his victim, a setup for the big grade con.

To be sure, identification, strategic support, and ingratiation are not only used in the grade game. These and other strategies are evident in additional con games, particularly those played by politicians, advertisers, salesmen, teachers, even panhandlers.

Panhandling for Fun and Profit: Another Con Game

You and your beloved are walking down the city's main drag on a sunny Saturday afternoon when the two of you are suddenly confronted by an hysterical young woman seemingly in a state of panic. Clutching what appears to be a crumpled doctor's prescription, she rambles that since she left her wallet at home she cannot purchase the medicine her diabetic husband so desperately needs. Weeping heavily, she pleads pathetically for five dollars, ostensibly the cost of the life-saving potion. Ms. Forgetful also swears that this act of kindness will be repayed as soon as she returns home. What would you do?

If her act was convincing, you would reluctantly dig into your wallet for a five spot. In truth, you have no choice in this situation, for the donation alleviates guilt feelings, the emotional state our panhandler so shrewdly evoked.[4]

Like most successful panhandlers, our counterfeit heroine realized that guilt can motivate a "lame" (potential donor) to produce "folding" money as long as the panhandler's plight is identifiable. Observes former university instructor Frederick Parr, now a successful panhandler in Chicago:

> "The lame has to think what it would be like if he was in that situation . . . I mean he (lame) has to empathize with the panhandler and realize that he could be in the same boat someday. That's why the con must at all times be convincing, believable, and plausible."[5]

To "score" (obtain money) it appears that the panhandler must utilize a guilt-producing identifiable con.

In addition to the preceding prescription routine, panhandlers employ other identifiable cons that are just as difficult to ignore. To illustrate this, consider the executive bathroom roll and the mugging scenario, two examples of panhandling artistry.

THE EXECUTIVE BATHROOM ROLL. Dressed in a blue pin-striped suit, the panhandler patiently waits near the entrance of the executive restroom in a large office building. On sighting an unsuspecting executive, the panhandler follows him into the frequently locked room whereupon he strikes up a friendly conversation with the lame. During their chat, the panhandler suddenly notices his wallet is missing. Seemingly worried, the well-dressed con man asks the executive to lend him fifteen dollars for a luncheon engagement with a vitally important client. Convinced the panhandler works in the building and is also an executive, the lame usually complies with the schemer's request. This identifiable con works about eighty percent of the time according to Parr.

MUGGING SCENARIO. This time the panhandler hits the streets with a ripped J. C. Penney suit, a blood-stained white shirt, a bruised face, and an anguished, frightened look. After carefully selecting a lame, the panhandler rapidly approaches him, indicating that he has just been mugged and needs five dollars for taxi fare to his daughter's wedding. In large cities where muggings are as common as McDonald's Big Mac, this type of plea, certainly an identifiable one, frequently meets with much success.

Now do you see what I mean by panhandling artistry? Why, the adroit con artist not only knows what to say but who to say it to. For example, in the mugging scenario and prescription routine, the panhandler prefers pitching couples, particularly male/female pairs. This preference is based on the assumption that women are more responsive to tales of woe than are men; consequently, the panhandler expects the female to cajole her male companion to provide the unfortunate victim with a generous payoff. In contrast, since unescorted women are reluctant to converse with strangers, they are more difficult to manipulate than are single males, according to many street husslers. Though these panhandling "truths" appear sexist, Parr argues that successful panhandlers, those earning at least $500.00 a week, cannot afford to disregard them.

Whom Do You Trust?

A society of husslers, we are selling our wares and ourselves daily. We take pride in our manipulative ability, frequently bragging about the unearned A, the way we conned the boss, and the line used to pick up Paulette. Similarly, we often admire those who secure promotions and large monetary payoffs through game playing. In fact, each year Americans purchase many books that promise them increased success in their daily manipulations. As American as apple pie, the con game is just another national pastime.

With this attitude, it is not surprising that we have difficulty trusting our fellow Americans, particularly advertisers, insurance-
men, politicians, lawyers, doctors, teachers, employers, salesmen,
judges. . . . ad infinitum. Similarly, is it any wonder that in relationships of intimacy we continue manipulating one another through
head games?[6]

HEAD GAMES

Like clockwork, little Aaron, a six year old, wakes up every Saturday
and Sunday morning at five o'clock, quietly tiptoes downstairs, and
gently turns on the high-powered quadraphonic F.M. radio to full
volume, literally blasting his parents out of bed. Upon hearing the
explosion of sound, Aaron's enraged father rushes downstairs and
screams at the child for disturbing another night's sleep. After dad

delivers a few stinging blows to Aaron's anatomy, the child returns to his room, only to engage in the same act the very next morning.

Aaron was playing the Disturbance Game, a well-orchestrated head game played by children who feel neglected. Although these kids frequently receive a swift kick in the pants for their efforts, this response, nevertheless, is a form of parental attention, the psychological payoff they so desperately need.

The Disturbance Game is just one of many head maneuvers in which children engage. Like adults, kids frequently resort to a head game when they find that a basic psychological need—affection, security, emotional support—is not being satisfied. Once a half-pint gamester successfully utilizes a head game, it is implanted deep in the psyche, "its (game) origin lost in the mist of time and ulterior nature clouded by social fog."[7]

It should come as no surprise that most head games we play as adults are simply extensions of those we initiated as young children. In fact, the transactional analyst, a therapist who specializes in remediating disruptive head games, often encourages patients to examine their early game playing experiences. This type of self-analysis frequently helps adult players understand the genesis of their gamey behavior, according to Eric Berne, the noted transactional therapist.

Focusing for a moment on adult gamesters, let's look at some of the head games in which you engage. Remember this one?

The Sexes at Play: Some Heavy Head Games

Jerry and Paula, both twenty years old, have been dating each other for almost a year. During this period, the lovebirds have manipulated each other on numerous occasions.

For example, Paula often feigned an illness while Jerry was visiting her. Though the complaint was usually minor—a headache, upset stomach, or a lower back pain—she watched Jerry closely as he responded to her spurious disorder. On other occasions, Paula indicated to Jerry that several "good-looking" males at school appeared as though they were strongly interested in her, another one of her gamey fabrications.

To be sure, Jerry was no paragon of honesty either. Occasionally, he purposely arrived for a date an hour or two late, expecting his beloved to be beside herself with worry. Instead, he frequently found her angry and upset which made him sorry he initiated the game.

Other times, Jerry was unusually quiet while in Paula's presence, ostensibly saddened by a passing thought. A patsy for the unhappy routine, Paula normally responded by looking searchingly into Jerry's doleful eyes and empathetically asking, "What's wrong, honey?" Staring into space, seemingly on the verge of tears, phony Jerry usually said, "Oh nothing; it's nothing. But thanks for

asking, baby."
No doubt about it, Jerry and Paula were two skillful gamesters.

CASE ANALYSIS. Sound familiar? At first glance, it may not. However, if you examine your own intimate relationship, you may discover that Paula and Jerry communicate much like you and your partner. Like our characters, the two of you have probably played the Reassurance Game—a psychological contest played by individuals who are unsure of each other's feelings.

The Reassurance Game can be played in several ways, as demonstrated by Paula and Jerry. For instance, in complaining of a physical discomfort, an example of what Berne calls the "sick" role, Paula was attempting to determine how Jerry felt about her. If he responded sympathetically, comforting her in this time of need, Paula might assume that Jerry cared for her. Conversely, she would naturally conclude that he was less than fond of her if his response was cold and indifferent. In short, Paula pretended to be sick in order to test Jerry's feelings—version number one of the Reassurance Game.

Version number two of the Reassurance Game occurred when Paula led Jerry to believe that several attractive males desperately sought her companionship. Expecting Jerry to become jealous, supposedly an indication of emotional commitment, Paula noticed his every expression as she related the spurious tale. If he appeared the least bit jealous, Paula would probably breathe a sigh of relief, while a cool, aloof response would most likely shatter her.

The final version of the Reassurance Game unfolded when Jerry purposely tried to worry his beloved. For example, by arriving for the date unusually late, he had hoped to evoke a worried response from Paula, ostensibly an expression of care and concern. Similarly, the despondent, sullen demeanor Jerry assumed at times was also supposed to elicit a concerned, affectionate reaction from his partner. Had Paula been unaffected by both situations, poor Jerry might have looked for another girlfriend.

By now, I suspect many of you have reflected on the last time you played the sickness, jealousy, and/or worry version of the Reassurance Game. Even though your beloved's reaction was never quite what you had expected, you still continue playing one or more versions of this head game. Why?

THE REASSURANCE GAME: AN EXERCISE IN FUTILITY. Like Jerry and Paula, we resort to the Reassurance Game when we are unable or unwilling to *directly* express our feelings to an intimate. In other words, when we fear a loved one will ignore our honest request for reassurance, we sometimes attempt to manipulate that person to secure the needed payoff. However, because we cajole our partner to reveal his or her feelings, we never know for sure whether the disclosure is authentic. A self-defeating ploy, the Reassurance Game frustrates the player and often weakens the relationship.

Before examining ways to reduce game playing, let's explore additional head games in which you participate.

Reflections on Transactional Analysis: "If It Wasn't for You."

Dating the same guy exclusively for the last four years, Esther, a junior in college, constantly complains about the relationship to a girlfriend. Having compromised her freedom so early, Esther regrets that she could not take better advantage of the rich resource of university males. "If it wasn't for my boyfriend," Esther argues, "I would have had a lot more fun in college. But you know Tom; he'd kill me if I looked at another guy."

More accurately stated, Esther *hopes* Tom would be furious if she dated another male. In truth, Esther is terribly insecure, so much so that she traded away her freedom for a steady date. Unable to cope with her insecure feelings, Esther unfairly blames Tom for her disappointing social life: "If it wasn't for him, I . . ." Clearly, Esther needs Tom more than she realizes.

You see, helpless, insecure, fearful Esther is actually behaving like a child, according to Eric Berne, the developer of transactional analysis (T.A.). It was the child in her that sought out a dominant individual like Tom on whom she could depend. In a psychological sense, Tom served as Esther's surrogate parent.

Commonly called "If It Wasn't for You," the preceding head game always follows the same pattern:

Characters—An insecure person seeks a domineering individual as a companion.

Psychological roles—Insecure individual plays the role of child; domineering person serves as a surrogate parent.

Payoff—Insecure individual is protected from the world that is feared and has someone to blame for feeling inadequate.

A common interpersonal game, it cannot be played unless each character assumes a certain psychological role which Berne calls an ego state.[8] In fact, the three ego states—parent, child, and adult—are largely responsible for most game playing, acccrding to proponents of transactional analysis. Let me elaborate.

Transactionalists claim that whenever we communicate, we display one or more of our ego states; that is, we behave as either a parent, child, or adult. As a parent, we are forceful, domineering, and accusatory. Unlike the parent, the child in us is spontaneous, immature, dependent, and helpless. Finally, we have the capacity to converse as an adult—rational, controlled, and objective. In Berne's view, game playing usually occurs when we fail to communicate as an adult but behave, instead, as a parent or child.

Unsurprisingly, we readily assume a parent or child ego state for a psychological payoff, the catalyst for each head game. For example, Esther's "child" was activated in "If It Wasn't for You" because she needed to be protected from the world in which she lived, indeed, a psychological payoff. In the game "Schlemiel," a party guest takes the role of child, constantly dropping objects and spilling drinks, to obtain forgiveness (payoff) from the host and others.[9] Starved for affection, the schlemiel thrives on such sympathetic responses as "That's O.K.," "Forget it," and "I understand." The reward for participating in a transactional game may be, among others, forgiveness, protection, vindication, justification, absolution, even self-castigation.

Because T.A. head games are so complicated, the players are often unaware of their ego states and potential payoffs. In fact, these individuals sometimes need extensive clinical treatment by a trained professional to uncover their motivations. Without proper care, T.A. gamesters will continue manipulating others, thus threatening the stability of each of their relationships.

Head to Head: Game Playing vs. Open Communication

Be it the Disturbance Game, Reassurance Game, "If It Wasn't for You," or "Schlemiel," each and every head game is self-defeating. In need of support from others, the players resort to deceptive psychological strategies to satisfy this psychological yen. However, their behavior only alienates those they meet, the gamesters' only source of need satisfaction. Hence, these type of people are frequently rewarded for their efforts with increased loneliness and frustration.

It seems, then, that a game-free encounter is in part based on open communication. Naturally, when individuals can freely share their feelings with others, requesting need satisfaction rather than securing it strategically, game playing is minimal. However, after years of playing games, people frequently have difficulty replacing their gamey behavior with honesty, as demonstrated in the final section.

BEYOND INTERPERSONAL MANIPULATION

It would be nice to end this chapter optimistically with an easy remedy for interpersonal manipulation. Why, I could suggest that con games would disappear if we were only more honest and candid with one another, but this may not be possible in a culture like ours where competition is revered. As long as we are compelled to "sell" ourselves to secure employment, attract a lover, or gain admittance to medical school, it is not likely we will dispense with our finely honed manipulative techniques.

In terms of head games, I could conclude, like many authors, that individuals will no longer engage in these psychological contests when they become more aware of themselves and others. However, this is easier said than done, for serious self-reflection is frequently a painful experience, one that most individuals will not endure. Moreover, since gamesters are often unaware of their manipulative tendencies, it generally surprises them to learn that their behavior needs to be modified. In short, head games may be difficult to eliminate.

It seems, then, that interpersonal manipulation is here to stay unless the culture is modified substantially, and its inhabitants radically alter their behavior. Unable to predict the future, I leave that to you.

SUMMARY

1. Individuals learn the value of interpersonal manipulation early in life from parents, siblings, and peers.

    As children, we were introduced to interpersonal manipulation through impression management—the art of constructing the most desirable public image. In time, we discovered that impression management can help us secure needed payoffs, including a date, a job, or a good grade.

2. An interpersonal game is a series of strategic moves used to secure an undisclosed payoff.

    Games have an ulterior quality, since the players conceal their motivations to ensure success. This type of maneuvering is widespread in America.

3. In a con game, the player uses certain manipulative strategies to secure a tangible payoff like a sale, a lower price, or a date.

    Reared in a competitive culture, individuals have no choice but to outmaneuver their competitors. By shrewdly employing strategic support, identification, and ingratiation, effective con game strategies, the gamester is frequently successful.

4. Head games are played for psychological payoffs—reassurance, self-castigation, vindication—and are thus more intricate than con games.

    Head games come in several varieties, including the Disturbance Game, Reassurance Game, and the many transactional games. Individuals resort to head games when they find that a basic psychological need—affection, security, emotional support—is not being satisfied.

5. Interpersonal games are self-defeating, for in the transaction the gamester often loses more than is gained.

Game players frequently alienate those they meet and are thus rewarded for their efforts with increased loneliness and frustration. Similarly, game playing is so pervasive in American society that many individuals have difficulty trusting even their most intimate companions.

PRACTICE CASE STUDY

Peering out the window of a new car dealership, Stan, a salesman for the company, spotted a young couple drive up in a battered 1966 Mustang. As Mac and his wife approached the front entrance, Stan readied himself for what he thought was a sure sale.

"How are you folks?" Stan warmly queried. "I'm Stan Pazazz, special sales consultant for Despicable Autos." Grasping Mac's hand firmly, Stan smiled broadly as the three exchanged social niceties.

"So how can I be of service to you folks?" Stan asked.

"Having heard so much about Despicable Autos," Mac replied, I thought we would see what it had to offer in the line of new cars. All we know for sure, though, is that we want something sporty."

Glib and self-assured, Stan praised them for their "intelligent" interest in a sports model. "You know," he said, "I could tell the minute I saw you that you were no ordinary customers; you had taste and style. You folks would only be satisfied with the sharpest auto Despicable carries—our special SS 11 Oleg Cassini Sport Coup."

Overwhelmed by the diamond studded wipers, mink hub caps, and satin upholstery, Mac passionately desired the SS 11 until he learned the price. At eight thousand dollars the dream car was much too expensive; Mac's wife did not agree.

"Oh honey," she pleaded, "if you bought me the car, I'd know you really cared! Oh, please, please!"

"Look Carol," he coldly responded. "We cannot afford it. Would you like me to go into debt for the next ten years?"

Rooting silently for Mac's wife, Stan realized he was about to lose the sale. In desperation, he said, "I know what you're going through, Mac. But I bought this car for my wife just last month to make her happy. It has improved our marriage immensely."

Shortly, Mac would be the reluctant owner of an Oleg Cassini Special.

EXPLORATORY QUESTIONS

1. Did the characters use impression management to manipulate one another?

2. Can you identify the con game strategies Stan used initially?

3. In pleading for the car, what type of head game was Carol playing?

4. What psychological roles did Carol and Mac assume during their brief argument?

5. What manipulative strategy did Stan use in his final attempt to sell the car?

6. Do you think Carol and Mac engage in many head games in their relationship?

7. Why do you suppose Mac finally capitulated to Stan and Carol?

ADDITIONAL PROJECTS

1. Imagine you are living in a game-free culture where honesty and authenticity are commonplace. Rewrite the preceding dialogue to reflect this cultural preoccupation.

2. If Mac and Carol came to you for marriage counseling, what advice would you give them about their head games?

INTERPERSONAL COMMUNICATION EXERCISES

1. Impression Management Exercise
   While conversing with others, we frequently engage in impression management. To find out just how pervasive impression management is, try this exercise.
   A. I want you to think about "you"; specifically, the you on a job interview, on a first date, in a classroom discussion, and in a conversation with your pals. Consider the way you manage your image in each of these situations.
   B. In a small group, share your observations about the images you maintain. Discuss the reasons why people engage in impression management.

2. Exercise in Transactional Analysis
   According to transactional analysis, each of us has three ego states—parent, child, and adult. Let's examine the ways these ego states operate in your life.

A. Select one relationship in which you have played head games. Identify the psychological role(s) you assumed in at least three of these head games. If you can, determine your motivation (payoff) for engaging in each game.

B. Share your observations with another person in the class. See if the two of you can help each other interact more honestly and directly in the future.

3. Con Game Exercise
   Con games are so common in the United States that we rarely examine them closely. Let's analyze a few con games through the following exercise.

   A. Teams of three to five members should select and examine a different con game. Identify the manipulative strategies used in one of the following games or examine a con game that is not on the list.
      1. The Insurance Game
      2. The Furniture Salesman Game
      3. The Funeral Business Game
      4. The Advertising Game
      5. The McDonald's Game
      6. The Supermarket Game
      7. The Men's Boutique Game

   B. After each team has thoroughly examined its topic, discuss the findings in class. Compare and contrast the many manipulative strategies used in each of these con games.

NOTES

[1] Erving Goffman, *Strategic Interaction* (University of Pennsylvania Press, 1969).

[2] Albert Scheflen, "Quasi-Courtship Behavior in Psychotherapy," *Psychiatry*, vol. 28 (1965), pp. 245–257.

[3] Farnum Gray, Paul Granbard, and Harry Rosenberg, "Little Brother Is Changing You," *Psychology Today*, March (1974), pp. 42–46.

[4] Information on panhandling derived from Robert Shuter, "The Persuasion of Panhandlers," Marquette University, 1975 (unpublished manuscript).

[5] Ibid., p. 5.

[6] Information about children and adult head games was partially derived from a study I conducted in the summer of 1974. See Robert Shuter, "The Head Game: Initial Speculations," Marquette University, 1974 (unpublished manuscript).

[7] Eric Berne, *Games People Play* (New York: Grove Press, 1964), p. 60.

[8] Ibid., pp. 23–28.

[9] Ibid., pp. 114–116.

CHAPTER 7

Uptight? Wanna Fight?
Conflict and Communication

"A bagel. Can you imagine fighting over a bagel? Believe it or not, my wife and I had an all-out battle the other night just because I accidentally ate *her* bagel.

"How was I to know it was hers? I didn't see my wife's initials on the surface; it didn't appear to be a woman's bagel. I mean, all bagels look alike, don't they?

"Why, the bagel seemed so pathetic sitting alone in that brown paper bag; I just couldn't ignore its doughy plea for love and affection. All the bagel wanted was to be reunited with its loved ones in the safe, dark cavern of my digestive tract. Who was I to deprive this bagel of family and friends?"

"A wise guy. I married a selfish wise guy. He knew that bagel was mine; who did he think hid the brown bag under the Hanes underwear?

"There he was gorging himself with the last bagel knowing full well that I had not consumed even a morsel of this Semitic delicacy. For sure, this bagel glutton has no concern for anyone else but himself."

Do you find this argument awfully petty and the characters terribly silly? Don't be too hard on our bagel connoiseurs, for you have also engaged in conflict with a lover, friend, or acquaintance over similar issues: the choice of a restaurant, the placement of furniture, the selection of a gift. Let's not forget the interpersonal battles fought over sex, love, and/or money—certainly all-time favorites for causing chaos. You and I spend much of our limited time on this earth fighting others; let's find out why.

TO BATTLE OR NOT TO BATTLE?

Everyone thought Bill and Jean were the ideal couple, destined for marital bliss after they graduate college. They thought alike, had similar interests, and never argued in public or private. In fact, Bill and Jean avoided discord like the plague, preferring to suppress angry feelings rather than express them. They were a top notch duo or so it seemed.

Whether they knew it or not, Jean and Bill had a problem— they wouldn't argue. Unwilling to engage in conflict, they were forced to conceal angry feelings which prevented them from really knowing one another; let me elaborate.

According to Bach and Deutch, individuals become acquainted with each other's thoughts and feelings through interpersonal conflict.[1] For example, during a combative encounter, people ventilate their angry feelings, revealing an important part of themselves to their partner. In addition, when tempers flare and teeth gnash, communicators often say things that have been bottled up inside of them for quite awhile. In the long run, these self-disclosures are important, for they help interactants better understand each other.

Similarly, conflict can also be a growth-producing experience, writes Thomas Oden, author of *Game Free: A Guide to the Meaning of Intimacy*.[2] Oden argues that during interpersonal conflict individuals frequently discover how their past behavior has affected their partner. For instance, communicators might learn that they are too domineering and do not provide their beloved with sufficient love and attention. These communicators now know in what ways they must change their behavior to improve the relationship; the next step is up to them.

Finally, interpersonal conflict can bring people closer together. Remember the last time you tried to convince your boyfriend to be more sensitive to your needs, and then there was the fight you had with your girlfriend because she was too possessive. In each case, the conflict eventually subsided and the two of you engaged in that age-old ritual of "making up." A mutual exchange of apologies, followed by a kiss and an embrace make this a very warm, intimate occasion, one that reunites the combatants emotionally. At times, it may have seemed worth fighting just to have the opportunity to make up.

Apparently, conflict can have a positive effect on a relationship.

However, once the combatants resort to verbal or physical abuse to win their argument, the confrontation can wreak havoc on the encounter.

HOW NOT TO BATTLE:
DIRTY FIGHTING

Though Hugh had neglected his studies the first semester at the university, this term he tried hard to secure good grades. He took careful notes in his classes, spent many hours in the library studying, and even hired a tutor to help him through a statistics course. Hugh was rewarded for his efforts at the end of the semester with satisfactory grades, a C+ average to be exact.

Arriving home for summer vacation, Hugh found his father waiting for him, report card in hand.

"Hugh, I warned you last semester not to bring home another lousy report card. Are you still playing big man on campus rather than studying for your courses?"

"No dad," Hugh whimpered, "I really tried my best this term."

"Then you just must be too stupid to get my money's worth out of college," dad angrily retorted. "I mean, a C+ average—any idiot could do better than that!"

On the verge of tears, Hugh wanted to defend himself but could not find the right words. Instead, he stared blankly at his father who continued the verbal assault.

"I was a great student in school. What the hell happened to you? You must take after your mother, dumb as they come!"

And on, and on, and on. . . .

CASE ANALYSIS. A bitter confrontation, it will not be quickly forgotten by either Hugh or his father. In fact, the two of them may not ever be close again, assuming, of course, that they once had a strong relationship.

Why was dad so angry with his son? On the surface, it appears that Hugh was attacked for receiving mediocre grades; however, daddy was actually upset because his little boy was not behaving as expected. That is, Hugh was not the successful, ambitious student his father had wanted him to be. Distressed that his son may not ever become a rich lawyer or doctor—a concern of many parents—dad vehemently attacked Hugh for disappointing him. Ostensibly fought over grades, the battle was actually waged for reasons that were never expressed during the confrontation which only complicated matters. Had dad tactfully disclosed what was troubling him, the conflict might have been resolved.

Rather than reveal his real concerns, father viciously maligned Hugh which intensified hostilities. Denounced and degraded, Hugh withdrew, unable and unwilling to express his angry, hurt feelings to his dad. Pop had successfully activated Hugh's defense system.

Defensive Communication

It was bad enough dad tried to impose his goals and desires on Hugh, that he refused to accept the son he supposedly loved. What made matters worse was the *way* he tormented Hugh, a classic example of what Jack Gibb calls *defensive communication.*[3]

Like all of us, Hugh prefers to think of himself as reasonably intelligent, sensitive, and industrious, a person of worth and significance. In calling Hugh stupid, dummy, and the like, dad was attacking his son's self-perceptions. Naturally, Hugh responded by defending himself; that is, he withdrew in the hope that father would end his tirade sooner. It didn't work; dad continued using negative evaluation—name calling, destructive criticism, even obscenities—to intimidate his son.

According to Gibb, negative evaluation is one of many types of communication that can elicit a hostile, angry response, commonly called a defensive reaction. In fact, Gibb argues that the listener will usually become defensive when the speaker appears superior, certain, apathetic, and/or manipulative. As with negative evaluation, each of these "messages" threatens an individual's self-perceptions.

For example, consider the last time your boyfriend was *certain* that his opinion, not yours, was absolutely correct. Surely, you wanted to bop him on the head, among other things. How about the ego maniacal professor who told your class repeatedly that he was *superior* to each and every student. Unsurprisingly, you would have stoned the professor if you thought your actions would not have hurt your grade. Let's not forget your *apathetic* girlfriend, the one who stared blankly at you after you poured your heart out to her. At that moment, you were hurt, angry, and dangerously close to strangling your beloved. Last but not least is mommy. That good-natured person, at times, tried to exert too much *control* over your life and even *manipulated* you on occasion to do what she felt was best; you resented her behavior more than she'll ever know. In each of these situations, you would have experienced varying degrees of anger and hostility because someone was trying to make you feel inferior and/or unintelligent.

Apparently, we should avoid communicating in ways that will elicit a defensive reaction from others. To accomplish this, each of us should communicate descriptively. That is, instead of "putting-down" an individual while arguing, we should attempt to *describe the action or behavior* that is upsetting us. An effective "fair fighting" method, descriptive communication is examined in detail later in this chapter.

Defensive communication is not the only way to cause interpersonal conflict and intensify it, as the following section demonstrates.

"I WIN, YOU LOSE": COMPETITION AND DISCORD

Scenario I

It's Thursday, the day of reckoning in History 101. You receive your test score and are surprised to learn that you earned a C even though you achieved an 80 on the exam. In talking to another student, you discover that the grading curve was high because three students, one of whom was your friend, had perfect test scores.

Be truthful, how would you feel about those students and, in particular, your friend?

Scenario II

Sam and his brother Al never got along; for some reason, they always bickered. Their relationship worsened when the two of them graduated college.

After graduation, Sam immediately secured a good job, while Al was forced to work as a stock boy in a local supermarket. Mom and dad did not help matters any, for each day Al was reminded by one or both of them that Sam was successful, implying, of course, that he was not. In fact, whenever the family had dinner together, Sam spoke freely about his "wonderful" position and Al remained strangely silent, at times, glaring at his successful brother.

Do these scenarios strike home? If they do then you can better appreciate just how destructive competition can be. It can dampen a perfectly fine relationship, as indicated in Scenario I, and/or further alienate individuals who have never been thrilled with one another, certainly the case in Scenario II. Why does competition frequently produce bitter, hostile confrontations?

In arguing that competition encourages us to thrive on the misery of others, Jules Henry, a noted anthropologist, provides some insight into the preceding question.[4] Essentially a brutal process, competition is really about winning and losing, according to Henry. As winners, we are exhilarated, while in losing each of us experiences humiliation, even misery. Knowing the price of losing, fearing failure, we strive desperately to win even though our success and subsequent joy is ultimately based on someone's misfortune. To illustrate Henry's theory, consider the "ooh" phenomenon.

Remember when your elementary school teacher asked the class a question? Invariably, thirty "oohing" and "ahing" students, each with his arm stretched out and wagging violently, competed for the teacher's attention. "Me, choose me, Mrs. Schmidt," "Please, oh pleeese," the kids supplicated until someone was finally chosen which caused the remaining students to moan like wounded animals. If the selected learner answered the question incorrectly, the moaning mob was elated, for each student had another chance to win Mrs. Schmidt's attention. To be sure, the class derived satisfaction from the failing student's embarrassment, humiliation, and misery.

While adults do not reveal their competitive sorrows and joys as conspicuously as children, grownups certainly experience the thrill of winning and the agony of defeat. Given the adversary nature of competition, it should come as no surprise that competing individuals often harbor hostile feelings for one another, even if the competitors happen to be close relatives. Returning to Scenario II for a moment, let's take a closer look at competition in the family, a common cause of interpersonal chaos.

Winning isn't everything?

Conflict Family Style: Sibling Rivalry

Al and Sam have probably been competing with one another since they were old enough to talk. As children, they competed for the highest grades and largest baseball trophy to gain mommy's and daddy's approval. In adulthood, Al and Sam continued trying to best each other in college and on the job. Simply put, their relationship suffered from a severe case of sibling rivalry, a most destructive form of familial competition.

As demonstrated in this scenario, parents frequently encourage siblings to compete with each other. For example, mom and dad often pit one child against the other to motivate their tots to behave properly and perform well in school: "Your brother can do it; why can't you?" "Look how nicely your sister is behaving today." "Why don't you take after your sister and study more?" Naive and impressionable, children heed these warnings to win their parents' support.

On other occasions, sibling rivalry is caused by factors over which the parents have little control. A young child, for instance, will often perceive a newborn brother or sister as a competitor no matter how hard mom and dad try to dispel this notion. Similarly, siblings sometimes compete for grades, girlfriends, and the like, though their parents may disapprove.

Apparently, sibling rivalry produces needless hostility and bitterness between those who are supposed to love one another. Families can do without this brand of competition.

Competition: A Final Note

While each and every competitive encounter does not always result in conflict, it should be understood that "any competition contains the seed for mutual hostility," according to Robert Nye, a social psychologist.[5] Though in theory human beings should be able to engage in "friendly" competition, it does not often work out this way, particularly if the reward for winning is attractive. To be safe, intimates or friends should not compete excessively with one another; instead, cooperation should be their goal.

Moving on to new territory, the following type of communication ought to be avoided if battling others is not your favorite activity.

DOMINATING YOUR WAY
TO HATRED AND HOSTILITY

Do Burt Reynolds, Ralph Nader, and Joe Namath have anything in common? No, they all don't have mustaches or wear panty hose. On the contrary, they probably dress differently, disagree on many issues, and wear dissimilar undergarments. What they do share, however, is their independent image; each of them supposedly says and does what he pleases. Convinced by the media that these are free-spirited souls, the public idolizes them for their candor and moxie.

Most of our heroes, both historical and media created, are independent people. This is not surprising given the value Americans place on individual freedom. On an interpersonal level, we frequently fight tooth and nail to maintain our freedom when it is threatened by those who attempt to dominate us. Consider.

While gathering my notes after class, I was approached by Rosemary, a shy, rather quiet student who rarely smiled.

"Dr. Shuter, could I talk to you for a moment?" she softly queried.

"Why sure Rosemary; what's up?"

Certainly, a great deal was up, for Rosemary began to cry almost immediately. Unsure what to say or do in these situations, I tried my best to calm Rosemary and find out what was bothering her.

"Dr. Shuter, it's my parents," lamented Rosemary. "They just won't accept the fact that I'm not fifteen anymore."

Relieved that my midterm test was not responsible for her tears, I listened intently as she explained her family problem.

"I have absolutely no freedom in that house. My parents tell me who to go out with, when to come home, what clothing to wear; I can't do anything without asking them first. God forbid if I argued with my mom or dad; I don't know what they'd do. I know I shouldn't be telling you this, Dr. Shuter, but I'm starting to *hate* my parents for treating me this way!"

CASE ANALYSIS. Can a child actually start to hate her mother and father just because they are too domineering? She sure can. What's more, a family can fall apart if parents usurp too much of their childrens' freedom, apparently the state of affairs in the preceding case.

Although Rosemary's parents probably thought their actions were in her best interests, they were mistaken. By strictly regulating Rosemary's life, they were alienating their child from them. To save the family, mom and dad must give their daughter some breathing room.

Rosemary's problem is not unique; in fact, many of you may resent your parents because they run your life. On occasion, you may have fought with mom and dad to regain your freedom only to find them stubbornly insensitive to your plight. At those moments, you contemplated leaving home for good, and maybe that's what you eventually did.

Regardless of the relationship, we resent being dominated. The boss who demands unquestioning obedience from the employees, the boyfriend or spouse who wants to control his beloved's life, and the male acquaintance who must have everything *his* way are equally repugnant to us. It appears that domination creates divisiveness and hostility, a prelude to bitter interpersonal conflict.

You Ain't Seen Nothin' Yet

By now, you should have gathered that defensive communication, competition, and domination can ruffle, provoke, or enrage a listener; however, this is only part of the story of interpersonal conflict. There is more to a hostile encounter than meets the eye, which brings us to another cause of discord: misperception.

MISPERCEPTION AND CONFLICT

Poor George is constantly being attacked, or so he thinks. His parents neglect him, uncles and aunts belittle him, friends turn on him, and girls put him down. There is simply no end to this abuse.

Why, just last week a girl refused to go out on a date with George; he blew his stack. Certainly, George could not forget his wealthy uncle who had the nerve to offer him a job at only twelve thousand dollars a year. Inexperienced, unemployed George was absolutely livid. Finally, there was his friend, Harold, who had the audacity to get married and "desert" George. He never forgave Harold for taking his nuptial vows.

Now do you understand why George fought bitterly with almost everyone? He had no choice; did he?

CASE ANALYSIS: PERSONALITY, MISPERCEPTION, AND CONFLICT.
Contrary to his beliefs, George had no reason to be hostile. His parents, relatives, and friends were not unusually cruel or insensitive; he just thought they were. No doubt about it, George's perceptions were quite distorted and his personality was to blame. Let me elaborate.

First, George did not like himself. He was dissatisfied with his physical appearance, unimpressed by his talents and skills, and disappointed with his intellect. Simply put, George had a poor self-concept, a topic closely examined in Chapter 2.

Like most individuals with a poor self-concept, George was convinced that everyone disliked him, a reasonable conclusion since George disliked himself. Because he perceived other people as critics, George naturally thought friends, relatives, and acquaintances were attacking him; in truth, they were not. Unsurprisingly, the misperceptions, hostile feelings, and unnecessary fights will continue until George thinks of himself in more favorable terms.

George was also afraid of people; the world and its inhabitants threatened him. Fearful of others, George imagined that everyone was abusing him, certainly a misperception. Evidently, George's fears involved him in as many needless conflicts as did his poor self-concept.

It seems, then, that individuals misperceive reality and start fights partly because of personality factors. In addition to personality, other elements produce misperceptions which frequently lead to interpersonal discord. Take trust, for example.

Trust, Misperception, and Conflict

Born and raised on the west side of Chicago, Darlene, a black student at a nearly all-white university, is constantly fighting with her white classmates and professors. While Darlene claims she does not like interpersonal discord, she always finds a reason to engage in conflict; a student verbally attacked her, a teacher dominated her, an administrator provoked her. "I gotta fight," she argues. "These honkeys are always getting on my case; I just can't *trust* them."

Darlene misperceived the words and actions of white folks; in fact, she viewed the constructive criticism of white students as verbal abuse, considered the teachers' directions as just another form of white domination; even harmless administrative memos provoked her. These misperceptions and needless conflicts occurred because Darlene distrusted Caucasians.

You see, interpersonal trust is based on expectation, according to Morton Deutch, a leading authority on trust behavior.[6] In trusting a person, we *expect* that individual to treat us with respect and sensitivity, to behave in a reliable, positive manner. In contrast, when we suspect an individual may not respond favorably to us— that we may be abused, exploited, or mistreated—we distrust that person. Because we *expect* to be treated poorly by those we distrust, we often misperceive their behavior, converting harmless words and actions into insults. Certainly, the preceding case demonstrates just how much distortion can occur when we distrust others.

To have a satisfying, harmonious relationship with a person, we must trust that individual. Once we seriously question a communicator's motives, we often misunderstand the person's behavior and conflict may result.

Evidently, we can misperceive ourselves right into a confrontation. When this occurs, we ought to know how to control the discord. Accordingly, the following section examines conflict management techniques.

ON MANAGING CONFLICT

How can you and I use interpersonal conflict to our advantage, maximizing its positive aspects and minimizing the negative effects? The answer seems to be in conflict management.[7]

In managing a conflict, one or more individuals attempt to effectively control interpersonal discord through the use of certain communication techniques. With these techniques, combatants can reduce the level of hostility, discover the reason for the conflict, and resolve their differences. Let's take a look at a few approaches to conflict management that can be used in daily encounters.

Ventilating Feelings: Telling It Like It Is

"Sure he tells me time and again that he cares about me, but actions speak louder than words. Anyone who could date a girl for three whole years and not marry her is certainly not desperately in love. I could tell him what's on my mind, but why do it; he'd only think I was an insecure nag. I'll give Myron another couple of weeks and then I'll tell him—I think."

Is Marianne gaining anything by hiding her feelings from Myron? She sure isn't; her frustration and hostility are growing with each passing day. Unable to keep these bitter feelings inside, Marianne finds herself picking on her sweetheart for petty issues—his selection of clothes, his walk, his hairstyle—instead of directly revealing her real concern: "Does Myron genuinely care about me?" Unsurprisingly, Marianne's testy mood and personal attacks have left Myron angry and confused.

This relationship is doomed unless Marianne ventilates her feelings; that is, she must tell Myron what's *really* bothering her. If she discloses her feelings, Marianne will no longer experience the bitterness and hostility that frequently result when communicators are reluctant to level with each other. In addition, ventilation will help Marianne and Myron iron out their differences, since a problem must be expressed in order to be resolved. Ventilation is an important conflict management technique.

Despite its potential advantages, ventilation can widen hostilities if the participants' disclosures are expressed defensively: "That was a stupid thing to do, you idiot!" To avoid this, the combatants should fight fairly, an effective method for ventilating feelings. Consider.

Fighting Fairly: Descriptive Communication

In a fair fight, the participants never berate, insult, or physically attack one another; instead, they *describe* the action or behavior that upset them. The key word here is describe, for communicators in a fair fight simply indicate *why* certain behaviors aroused them rather than denounce each act as irrational or ridiculous. To fight fairly, then, individuals must discuss the *cause* of the conflict without negatively evaluating either the other person or his/her behavior. For example, take my wife and me.

Though we sometimes have heated arguments, this time we had a fair fight. Instead of verbally or physically attacking each other, we tried to ventilate our feelings in a constructive manner.

ROBERT *(looking at his wife):* What's wrong with you, Diana? Why are you so down?

DIANA: Believe it or not, I'm still upset with the way you treated me last night at the party.

ROBERT *(getting angry):* What did I do that was so wrong?

DIANA: Before you fly off the handle let me tell you how I feel. First, you spent almost the entire evening with that grad student; I felt as though you were ignoring me. Then you left the party for over an hour without even telling me; again you upset me. I couldn't help feeling angry and hurt all evening.

ROBERT: I guess I did spend quite a bit of time away from you last night, but you know how much I enjoy talking to people. I didn't mean to hurt you. I'm sorry.

I had not intended to upset my wife at the party; however, I quickly discovered *why* my behavior angered her. And because she described what aroused her without denouncing me or my actions, I did not lose my temper. Diana had ventilated her feelings without increasing hostilities, a successful example of fair fighting.

Might, Flight, Fair Fight

As you well know, whenever tempers rise, self-control diminishes; we often say and do things which we later regret. Unsurprisingly, we are not capable of fighting fairly in the heat of passion.

When voices blare and bodies stiffen, it is wise, then, to *flee* from the situation before "might makes right!" That is, the warring parties should separate until hostilities die down, with each person, for example, withdrawing to different sections of the house or apartment. During this cooling off period, individuals frequently regain their composure, a requirement for fair fighting. Two people are often ready to fight fairly after only a brief separation.

Apparently, voluntary separation, otherwise referred to as *strategic flight,* is an important conflict management technique; it can even save lives. For example, police officers are sometimes maimed or killed when they attempt to resolve a family conflict while the individuals are still enraged with one another. If police officers remembered to separate angry combatants before attempting to mediate the encounter, fewer officers would be hurt.

In sum, fair fighting can only take place when the participants are ready, willing, and able to calmly describe what angered them. To achieve this, individuals in conflict often have to separate for a few minutes, hours, even days.

Conflict Management: A Final Word

In all honesty, conflict management is easier said than done. Why? Because individuals are rarely concerned about reconciliation or the methods for achieving it when they are angry at someone. Instead, each combatant is usually preoccupied with winning the battle; nothing else seems to matter. Nevertheless, all of us should strive to manage our conflicts, for it is the only productive way to fight.

CONFLICT, CONFLICT, CONFLICT

By now, you should have gathered that conflict in itself is not disastrous; it is the *way* we engage in discord that creates problems. Knowing this, each of us should avoid fighting dirty and instead battle fairly. In so doing, we will reap the benefits of interpersonal conflict, a potentially growth-producing experience.

SUMMARY

1. Interpersonal conflict can have a positive effect on a relationship.
   Conflict can be a growth-producing experience for the participants. It can also bring people closer together.

2. Certain types of conflict can wreak havoc on an encounter.
   Defensive communication frequently causes bitter conflict. Interpersonal discord is also intensified through competition and domination.

3. Interpersonal conflict is often the result of misperception.
   Individuals frequently misperceive reality when they distrust others and/or have a poor self-concept. These misperceptions sometimes lead to unnecessary interpersonal conflicts.

4. Interpersonal discord should be controlled through conflict management techniques.
   Ventilating feelings, fair fighting, and strategic flight are reasonably effective ways to manage conflict. These approaches can diminish interpersonal hostility and even reconcile angry communicators.

5. Conflict management is easier said than done.
   When individuals are angry, they are rarely concerned about reconciliation or the methods for achieving it. For this reason, conflict management is sometimes difficult to accomplish.

PRACTICE CASE STUDY

Twenty years old and college juniors, Paul and Sara decided one weekend to get engaged. Though the engagement was to last until they both graduated from school, Paul wanted to make a formal announcement to friends and relatives as soon as possible. Without consulting Sara, Paul decided to have a party at which time their marital intentions would be disclosed. Sara did not like the idea; however, she raised no objection, for fear of angering Paul.

Almost immediately, Paul went to work planning the party. He selected the guests, the day of the event, and the site for the festivities: Sara's apartment.

Upon learning of Paul's plans, Sara exploded: "To be honest, I think your arrangements are ridiculous. Only a genius business administration major like yourself could have dreamed up this crummy party."

Surprised and angered by Sara's remarks, Paul responded, "Hey, I worked hard on planning this party. You sure as hell couldn't have done any better, Miss Home Economics major."

"Don't scream at me," Sara bitterly replied. "I'm not your wife and I don't know whether I ever want to be!"

With that, Paul stormed out of the apartment and Sara began to cry.

EXPLORATORY QUESTIONS

1. In your estimation, what made Sara angry initially?

2. Why didn't Sara ever confront Paul with her real concerns?

3. Why did Sara's outburst only intensify hostilities?

4. Did Paul's response to Sara also aggravate the situation? Why?

5. Do you think this conflict can be reconciled? How?

ADDITIONAL PROJECTS

1. Explain how conflict management techniques could be used to diminish hostilities.

2. By rewriting the dialogue, convert this hostile encounter into a fair fight.

INTERPERSONAL COMMUNICATION EXERCISES

1. To find out just how destructive defensive communication can be, try this exercise.
   A. Next time you communicate with someone display one or more of the following behaviors: neutrality, superiority, certainty, and negative evaluation. Note the individual's verbal and nonverbal reactions.
   B. After the two of you have conversed for awhile, ask your partner if he/she was annoyed by your communication style. Develop conclusions about defensive interaction, and discuss them in class.

2. To theorize about fair fighting is easy; doing it is another story. Experiment with fair-fighting techniques through the following exercise.
   A. With another person, role-play the following scenarios. Avoid

evaluative statements; be as descriptive as possible while ventilating your feelings.

1. You have discovered that your girlfriend/boyfriend has been secretly dating your best friend. Disclose your feelings to your girlfriend/boyfriend in a descriptive manner.
2. Your sister/brother has lifted five dollars from your wallet without asking. Ventilate your angry feelings.
3. You are angry with your father because he has warned you once again to stop going out with your boyfriend/ girlfriend.

3. Can competition produce hostility and bitter interpersonal discord? Let's find out.
   A. Select a married male and a married female to interview. Ask each individual to react to the following hypothetical situations. Note their reactions. What conclusions can you draw about the relationship between competition and discord?

   Pose these hypotheticals to a married male:
   1. Your wife has just secured a new job. It's similar to yours except that she has more responsibility than you and is paid a higher salary. Would you feel like you were competing with her? If so, how might this affect your relationship?
   2. You and your best friend are in line for an important promotion. Only one of you can get the position. Do you think the competition will affect the way you communicate with one another?

   Pose the following to a married female:
   1. You've discovered that your husband thinks your best girlfriend is very attractive. When she comes over next week for dinner, do you think you will have any difficulty communicating with her?
   2. You're in love with your new job, so much so that you spend ten hours a day and many weekends at the office. Would your husband resent competing with your job for your attention? How would your relationship be affected by these circumstances?

NOTES

[1] George R. Bach and Ronald M. Deutch, *Pairing* (New York: Avon Books, 1970).

[2] Thomas Oden, *Game Free: A Guide to the Meaning of Intimacy* (New York: Harper & Row, 1974).

[3] Jack Gibb, "Defensive Communication," *Journal of Communication,* vol. 3 (1961), pp. 141–150.

[4] Jules Henry, *Culture Against Man* (New York: Random House, 1963).
[5] Robert Nye, *Conflict Among Humans* (New York: Springer-Verlag, 1975), p. 88.
[6] Morton Deutch and Robert Kraus, *Theories in Social Psychology* (New York: Basic Books, 1965).
[7] Additional information on conflict management can be found in George Bach and Peter Wyden, *The Intimate Enemy* (New York: William Morrow), 1969; Thomas Oden, *Game Free: A Guide to the Meaning of Intimacy* (New York: Harper & Row, 1973).

CHAPTER 8

Prisoners All:
Social Context and Communication

Abbie Hoffman, former leader of the Yippie Party, was interviewed several years ago by David Frost. During the encounter, Hoffman disclosed that he was a free human being, liberated from all societal constraints, able to say and do what he pleased. After making the statement which, incidentally, was grammatically correct and punctuated by several well-placed American gestures, Abbie, sitting about three feet from Frost, glanced at his watch, indicating to David that it was time for him to leave. Whether he knew it or not, Hoffman was faithfully abiding by the communication rules of American culture.

Seemingly the paragon of human liberation, Abbie was actually a prisoner of social context. His language, distance at which he interacted, gestures displayed, and the signal used to close the conversation were all very American. In fact, his every word and movement was influenced in some way by several environments, including his culture, ethnic group, social class, and region of the country. Abbie was not as free as he thought.

Like Abbie Hoffman, we too are captives of the environments in which we live. Each of these environments influences our communication more than most of us realize. Consider the following.

CONTEXT AND COMMUNICATION: AN INTRODUCTION

Several Midwesterners visiting New York City decided to lunch at Stage Delicatessen in the heart of Manhattan. Entering the restaurant at noon, they found themselves in the middle of a stampeding human herd crying out for corned beef, pastrami, and potato salad. Wanting to leave but swept up by the crowd, the group slowly approached the water hole where they were greeted by the mellifluous tones of Joe Schwartz, the owner of Stage.

"How many hillbillies are there in your group?" mused Joe. Stunned by the remark, the group stared curiously at him.

"You people too loaded down with souvenirs and New York City tee shirts to talk?" razzed the proprietor.

Visibly disturbed by his question, Millie, the most aggressive of the group, nervously responded that there were three people in her party. At which point, Joe, holding back a smile, strongly suggested that they lunch at a local hotdog stand.

Before the group was able to determine whether he was serious, the proprietor unexpectedly commanded them to collect their souvenirs and head rapidly for three empty chairs in various sections of the restaurant.

"But we would like a table for three," squealed Millie.

"Hey, I don't need a headache," responded Joe. "Just get your fannies to those seats and have a nice lunch."

CASE ANALYSIS: "WAS THAT GUY AN ANIMAL OR DO THEY ALL TALK LIKE THAT?" All the way home to Nebraska, Millie and her friends probably talked about the unfriendly, insensitive, even brutal treatment they received from Joe. Assuming that all city dwellers are much like the king of the corned beef sandwich and dill pickle, the group may have charged New Yorkers with being cold and uncaring. What they did not understand was that Joe's behavior was an expression of love, not hate—that the repartee was not intended to be abusive but rather an attempt to establish rapport.

Joe's behavior was not unusual; in fact, it is a customary and expected form of interaction in the Big Apple. An extension of the New York City "rank"—a verbal game during which two kids playfully denigrate each other's mother—Joe's friendly abuse is as much a part of the city as the United Nations. Unaware that the deli owner's put-downs were meant to serve a positive function, the Midwesterners inaccurately concluded he was unusually hostile.

The unique communication system of New York City, its warm put-ons and playful verbal combat, is often threatening to the unsuspecting visitor. Yet, this city is no different than Atlanta, Des Moines, Milwaukee, or, for that matter, any population center, since they all have distinctive verbal and nonverbal communication patterns. In fact, in every city and nation, culture and ethnic group, the inhabitants share certain language patterns and bodily movements. Accordingly, the words we use, movements we make, and meanings we bring to someone else's communication are greatly influenced by social context.

A Final Look at Joe and Millie

Jean Piaget, the noted psycholinguist, and Ray Birdwhistell point out that verbal and nonverbal communication are learned behaviors, acquired from culture, social class, ethnic group, and regional affiliation.[1] In fact, these environments even influence our gestures, tactile behavior, and the way we "share" our eyes during a conversation. And because each environment has its own communication customs, individuals from different cultures, ethnic groups, and regions of a country frequently misunderstand one another.

In spite of what some of you may still be thinking, Joe, the pastrami king, was not born with cold water in his veins nor is Millie necessarily a warm, sensitive Midwesterner. Instead, both are probably caring, understanding people who communicate in similar though very different ways, with Millie reflecting the passive, soft-spoken ethos of the Midwest and Joe an extension of New York City—aggressive, forceful, and dominant. To impose an ethical judgment on either communication style is ludicrous since both are appropriate for their respective regions. However, evaluation always occurs and confrontations sometimes ensue when individuals reared in different social contexts interact. This is readily apparent when people from different cultures are unfamiliar with one another's communication customs.

CULTURE AND COMMUNICATION: A STICKY ISSUE

Culture has been defined as customs, values, and beliefs transmitted from generation to generation. It is that which supposedly makes the French so amorous, the Italians so emotional, and the English so proper. While every society has a dominant culture that houses its distinctive characteristics, so, too, are there subcultures (i.e., Italian-Americans, black-Americans, etc.) within a dominant culture.

Culture is also the foundation of human interaction. That is, every aspect of our communication—the way we open and close a conversation, our language and nonverbal behavior—is a reflection of the culture. It also controls our words and body movements, dictating the appropriate behavior for each situation and person. Without question, culture has more influence on interpersonal communication than all other social contexts.

"Whatsa Matta?" A Cultural Clash

Meet Luigi Giovianni, Milwaukee's newest addition to the Italian-American community. Born and raised in Venice, Italy, Luigi, twenty-two years old, moved to this conservative midwestern city at the insistence of his father's American friend, Sam Czwicki.

Some Milwaukeeans still talk about the row that developed when Luigi, dressed in revealing tight pants, shirt opened almost to the waist, and purse in hand, arrived at the airport in beer town U.S.A. Shocked at Luigi's appearance, Sam, the brewery worker, was speechless while the former gondolier, overwhelmed by excitement, hugged and kissed the friend he had never met. After his emotional explosion, Luigi, sensing something was wrong, asked his Polish host what was troubling him. Sam, an unusually direct man, responded bluntly that Luigi dressed, moved, and acted like a woman. A verbal battle ensued followed by a fist fight, resulting in the incarceration of Luigi and Sam charged with disorderly conduct.

CASE ANALYSIS. Can you blame Sam Czwicki for concluding that Luigi was effeminate? Reared in the Midwest, the heartland of America, Sam was taught that men are not supposed to carry a purse, wear clinging apparel, and freely emote in the presence of females and especially other males. Like many Americans, Sam quickly pins the "fag" label—a euphemism for homosexual—on males who excessively embrace or touch other men and/or display too much emotion in public. Unknowingly, Luigi had violated fundamental rules of American sex role behavior.

On the other hand, can you blame Luigi for defending his masculinity? A "machismo" culture where males pride themselves on female domination, Italy produces men who are very much caught up in their own masculinity. In fact, it is not uncommon for an Italian man to publicly seduce and touch an unescorted female with whom he is unfamiliar. Because of centuries of conditioning that females desire to be controlled by men, the Italian male is most persistent, wheedling the female with amorous overtures far beyond the termination point for his American counterpart.

The appearance of the Italian male also reflects the chauvinism of the culture. The garb—pants and shirt that fit snugly emphasizing the physique, buttocks, and groin—is worn by many Italians until they feel their bodies are no longer attractive, which may be fifty, sixty, even seventy years old. Naked without his black or tan purse in which he carries cigarettes, hair brush, and other personal items, the Italian man is rarely seen without one. Rather than communicating that the wearer is a homosexual, the uniform is supposed to convey that the Italian male is virile, an expert in matters of sexuality.

So when Sam Czwicki criticized Luigi's clothes, he was challenging his masculinity, a stunning emotional blow for someone preoccupied with his maleness. More importantly, Sam's evaluation of Luigi's appearance was incorrect; the Italian was no more effeminate than his Polish-American host. Because his criticism of Luigi's apparel was based on American standards, it's no wonder an Italian John Wayne was mistaken for an American "fag." Evidently, clothing—its color, design, even fit—is a communication vehicle. Reflecting the values of the culture, outward appearance clearly communicates different meanings in different societies, particularly in the case of social systems (i.e., Italy and America) that have dissimilar regulations regarding appropriate male and female behavior.

Furthermore, Czwicki misinterpreted his guest's penchant for physical contact. Though Sam was astonished with the manner in which Luigi emoted—gesturing wildly, embracing, and constantly touching—his behavior is commonly accepted, even expected in Italy. In fact, while conducting a communication study in Italy, I discovered that males are extraordinarily tactile, freely touching and embracing one another during a conversation.[2] They also use many gestures while talking, some short and jabbing, others wild and expansive. Marked by dramatically presented narratives, much embracing and holding, constant movement of the body and limbs, and loud, emotional outbursts, a typical discussion between two Italian males is a sight to behold. In a culture where emotion is regarded highly, where reason is less important than love and passion, one might expect Italian men to communicate as they do.

Luigi was framed by social context. While appropriate for Venice, his behavior violated American communication rules which strictly regulate touching and display of emotion between males. Because Sam was unfamiliar with Italian customs, he used American standards to evaluate Luigi's behavior. However, had both of them been aware of each other's cultural values, this crisis could have been averted.

CULTURAL VALUES: THE BUILDING BLOCKS OF COMMUNICATION

Each culture has certain preferences concerning the way human beings ought to behave. Commonly called values, they are imposed on us as children and are supposed to guide and direct our behavior. In the preceding case, for example, Luigi's appearance and communication style reflect the value that Italians place on emotionality and male domination. Similarly, Sam's criticism of his guest was motivated by the American notion of the rational male, always in control of his emotions. The confrontation, then, was actually precipitated by differing cultural values.

To help examine cultural values, Condon and Yousef, noted authorities on intercultural communication, developed a list of conditions which they believe people in all societies encounter.[3] Arguing that a culture has a certain orientation for each of these conditions, Condon and Yousef attempt to identify several *value orientations*. For example, they indicate that cultural values focus on such universal societal conditions as age, sex, and activity. On closer examination, one finds that a society either values the young, middle-aged, or the old, puts a premium on equality of the sexes, female or male superiority, and qualifies as a "doing" or "being" culture. Each of these is a value orientation and exerts a substantial influence on communication.

The United States, for instance, is clearly a "doing" culture, since productivity, efficiency, and the acquisition of material goods are paramount. Unlike the United States, Mexico, a "being" culture, emphasizes self-fulfillment often at the expense of productivity. Since most Americans are unaware that in a "being" culture time is not watched but enjoyed, they often conclude that Mexican workers are lazy and unintelligent. Similarly, a surprisingly large number of Mexicans visiting the United States feel that Americans are cold and insensitive simply because they are always doing (producing) something, having little time for a friendly chat. If more Americans and Mexicans were aware of one another's activity orientation, such inaccurate interpretations might be prevented.

You should have gathered by now that communication patterns can be better understood by examining cultural values. Furthermore, value analysis can frequently help one reconcile cross-cultural breakdowns and even avert such crises. Relying heavily on the value orientation approach, the following case demonstrates the tight relationship between values and communication.

Arabic and American Communication: A Case of Value Differences

I met Habib in Bagdad, Iraq, while on a tour of the Arabic countries. We had much in common; he was a professor of communication sciences at the local university and I a struggling graduate student in the same field. We immediately became friends.

During my two week visit we spent quite a bit of time together discussing our mutual interests. I learned that Habib lived in a small town outside Bagdad with his grandparents, parents, and two single sisters. Interested in visiting an Iraqi home, particularly one inhabited by two eligible young women, I hinted to Habib on several occasions that I wouldn't turn down a dinner invitation. However, I never received one nor did I learn much more about his sisters than their ages and marital status.

At first it bothered me that Habib did not extend an invitation to visit his home. I pondered the issue unemotionally and concluded that formally opening one's house to a stranger was not necessary in Iraq. So one evening after dinner I payed Habib an unexpected visit only to discover my conclusion could be no farther from the truth.

"Robert, what brings you so suddenly to my home?" said Habib, appearing startled and nervous.

Uneasy because I had invaded his privacy, I stammered through the clumsy American excuse for the uninvited visit. "Well, I was in the neighborhood and thought I would drop by."

"Please come into my modest home," responded Habib as he reached for my arm. He then led me into a large, ornate room packed with what appeared to be every prized possession the family owned—statues, paintings, glassware, and china.

Desiring to meet his parents and especially his sisters, I asked to see the rest of the house after being isolated in the room for over an hour with Habib. Surprised and seemingly angered by the request, Habib quickly responded that it was not possible and then excused himself, leaving the room in a huff. Had I insulted him, wounded his pride? Habib's reaction was a mystery.

Then I committed the cardinal crime. Soon after he left, I realized that if I did not find a toilet immediately Habib's showroom would have an unwanted addition. My anxieties surfaced: Would Habib mind if I went to the toilet without asking him? Kidneys exploding, having no alternative, I ventured out of the room in search of the water closet. I found myself in a long hallway with several doors leading to various rooms in the house. As I was gently opening the second door and about to peek in, Habib's voice rang out angrily from the end of the hall.

"Robert, what are you doing out of the front room? Please return before the women are disturbed."

"But Habib I have to use the toilet!" I yelped in pain.

"You must return to the room immediately. I will guide you to the water closet when things are arranged," Habib demanded.

Patience worn thin, unable to contain my anger, I stormed out of the house muttering an ancient Brooklyn curse. I never saw Habib again.

CASE ANALYSIS. The confrontation could have been avoided and our friendship sustained had I been familiar with several Arabic values. I had violated a host of communication rituals that were an outgrowth of Iraqi culture. Let me explain.

My first transgression was the uninvited visit to Habib's home. His look of amazement is no longer a mystery after learning that in Iraq the home is reserved for family, relatives, and close friends, open only on special occasions to invited strangers and acquaintances. An invitation to visit and dine is an expression of deep friendship, a relationship Habib and I had not developed. Similarly, the infraction was of a serious nature because it occurred within a culture that values formalism.

Unlike the United States in which informality is encouraged and "rules are made to be broken," Arabic cultures revere custom and ritual, and demand unquestioning obedience of the law. This preoccupation with formalism is extended into the home where the husband functions as benevolent dictator, children and women are seen but not heard, and guests *never* visit unless invited. That is, all the relationships in the home are strictly regulated by rules to which inhabitants, friends, and strangers must adhere. Having violated the formalism of the Iraqi household, my unexpected appearance at Habib's door probably communicated to him that I was either exceedingly strange, as civil as a rhinocerous, or experiencing a psychological crisis for which I needed immediate consolation.

A VICTIM OF CIRCUMSTANCE. However eccentric I appeared in Iraq, my behavior was motivated by the American value of informality. Stressing open and honest communication, the American culture encourages individuals "to be themselves," to express their feelings and thoughts. Status façades, like hiding behind the mask a professional title provides, are usually not accepted. Similarly, pomp and circumstance is generally frowned upon except on certain special occasions like weddings and anniversaries. Informality is also reflected in the English language which provides only one form of the pronoun "you" when referring to both strangers and intimates. Most cultures have two forms—the formal "you," an indication of respect, and the familiar "you," a sign of friendship.

In view of my value training, communication specialists will surely find me a victim of circumstance. Reared in a culture where friends and neighbors freely pop in on one another—an additional manifestation of American informality—it did not occur to me that my unannounced visit would violate the Iraqi ethic of formalism. Similarly, my American values did not help me understand the treatment I received in Habib's home.

HOW NOT TO MAKE YOURSELF AT HOME IN IRAQ. To provide an environment in which visitors "feel at home" is an American custom, one that is also founded on informality. Translated into specific behaviors, this custom permits guests to serve themselves and have access to most rooms in the house, especially the bathroom.

In Arabic societies, however, one does not "make oneself at home" while visiting. In fact, guests never serve themselves and are supposed to remain in the room in which they are seated, leaving only with the permission of the host who then guides the visitor to the destination, be it bathroom or front door. Certainly appropriate by American standards, requesting a tour of the house and leaving a room unescorted by the host are disrespectful and most insulting to an Arab.

Having breached Iraqi amenities, Habib's angry reaction should no longer be puzzling. Still, his customs seem strange unless one also understands the function of status and the role of men and women in Arabic culture.

Surely, any advertising executive would be awed by the way each Arab household creates and maintains its status image. Somewhat like America, Arabic societies encourage families to display their material possessions in order to communicate their status to others. Reminiscent of the American bourgeoisie, the typical Arabic home has a special room in which every valuable possession is conspicuously displayed. Unlike even the richest American household, however, guests are forbidden to see all but this room until they are accepted as intimate family friends. This status façade is maintained by permitting guests to leave the showroom only after, as Habib said, "arrangements have been made." This includes making sure the hall is clean, doors are closed, and the rest of the family, especially the women, are not in sight. Accordingly, my unescorted tour of Habib's home tarnished the family's image and impugned the integrity of his two sisters.

HOW NOT TO MEET A WOMAN IN IRAQ. Males dominate every Arabic institution, from government to the home. In fact, the woman's place is *only* in the home in which she learns as a child to be passive and servile, shy and naive. A single woman, for example, is not supposed to talk to unfamiliar males, nor is she to be seen by strange men visiting her parents, with whom she must live until married. To meet an unattached female, a man must contact an intermediary who consults with the woman's family before arranging a closely watched rendezvous. Females who violate these customs compromise their moral integrity, and brothers disgrace themselves when they permit their sisters to stray from the righteous path.

In retrospect, by requesting to meet his sisters, I was unknowingly communicating to Habib that I did not care about their integrity or his. Further, my unannounced walk through his home was even more threatening since I might have accidentally met the women. Had that occurred, I would have communicated to Habib that I considered his sisters to be no better than prostitutes. Though terribly innocuous in Brooklyn, my behavior, when evaluated by Arabic standards, was most offensive, producing a bitter, hostile response from Habib.

A Concluding Statement:
Values and Communication

By now you should appreciate the close relationship between communication and cultural values. Indeed, human interaction is linked to value orientations about such issues as formalism, sex roles, and status. And because values differ from culture to culture, the meaning associated with a particular behavior also varies. That is, a request to see a friend's home communicates disrespect in a culture founded on formalism, but conveys a positive feeling in a society like ours where informality preeminates.

While tourists visiting a foreign country are not expected to be anthropologists, a basic awareness of major cultural values will help them understand the behavior of others and the way others perceive them. However, because each society has many value orientations, one cannot be cognizant of all or even most of them. In addition to increasing our awareness of cultural values, we should familiarize ourselves with the society's communication rules and rituals, its situational proprieties.

COMMUNICATION RULES

Erving Goffman, sociology's astute observer of human interaction, coined the term *situational propriety* which he defines as a rule that regulates the communication occurring within a particular social setting.[4] One Iraqi situational propriety, for example, prevents females from having unfamiliar males visit them at home (social setting). In Italy, most social settings have situational proprieties that encourage males to touch and embrace each other when greeting and/or departing. And when attending a funeral (social setting) in the United States one is supposed to walk slowly, appear sad, and use appropriate corpse rhetoric: "He looks so lifelike." "He was such a good man." "He seems at peace." Be it funeral or wedding, housewarming or courtship, each social situation is governed by communication rules which reflect values derived from the culture.

One can learn the communication proprieties for each setting without understanding the underlying societal values. For example, a person can know that the rules of courtship in America require men to initiate conversations with women, and never realize that they are an extension of cultural values concerning male/female sex roles. Accordingly, interpersonal communication can be enhanced by familiarizing oneself with situational proprieties.

Moving on, let's find out how people become acquainted with the rules of communication.

Kids Say the Darndest Things: Learning the Communication Rules

Art Linkletter amassed a fortune by cajoling young children to say things that should not have been voiced in front of a television camera. Aware that children freely violate the communication rules of each setting, Linkletter's prodding frequently resulted in disclosures that must have made the kids' parents feel like moving to another planet. Certainly, when some of these children arrived home after the show, mommy and daddy strongly indicated to them that they better learn the rules of the communication game before they make their next public appearance. Parents, then, are primarily responsible for teaching children the appropriate language and nonverbal behavior for each social setting.

Regardless of culture, familiarizing children with situational pro-

prieties—"harnessing" them to social context as Goffman puts it—
begins as soon as the infant is aware of the environment. The child's
first lessons are always about the family setting.

Looking down at their child in the crib, the parents repeat over
and over that the balding chap with the expanding girth is "dada,"
and the weary person with the artificial smile is "mama." Constantly
bombarded by these words, the infant not only learns who these
adults are but the proper way to refer to them. He generally receives
the same treatment from visiting grandparents, uncles, and aunts,
and in time will recognize that these people are his family and
should be treated in a very special way. When Johnny wiggles,
beams, and coos at his parents, it communicates to them that he
has finally internalized his first communication lesson. Johnny is now
partially harnessed to the family setting.

As he grows up, the harness is fastened securely to Johnny. Remember those infamous parental warnings regarding the proper
way to communicate in the home? "Don't talk back to your mother."
"Your sister is a girl, treat her that way." "That type of language
will not be tolerated in this house." "Look at your father when
he's talking to you." Then there were the communication rules of
public places: restaurants, parks, museums, libraries, and theaters.
We learned them all from parents, other adults, and peers.

If the culture is successful, the individual knows at least by age
ten what the communication expectations are for most social situations. With this knowledge, the communicator can use the body
movements, speech, gestures, even tone of voice that the setting
requires. Harness firmly in place, one can finally take part in the
drama of human interaction.

THE PARTY

A One-Act Play

Produced and written by		Directed by
THE CULTURE		PARENTS AND PEERS
	Starring	
	YOU	

The play takes place in any middle class apartment in any section
of the United States. Like all dwellings inhabited by young people,
it is modestly decorated—Dali and Picasso prints on the walls, a
sofa, a few chairs, and a vinyl covered bar with a sign above it
that reads "Booze Cures All That Ails." Some of the lights are turned
off to create a relaxed mood, and a jazz/rock album, probably Chick
Corea or Herbie Hancock, is playing in the background. People

are milling throughout the apartment, each person clutching a drink.

As the scene opens, you have just entered the apartment and are speaking to the hostess.

HOSTESS *(bouncy and beaming):* I'm glad you were able to come. Did you have any difficulty finding the place? We're a little off the beaten track.

GUEST *(cool and pleasant):* Not really, Bill Schmidt gave me the directions. He's been to several of your parties.

HOSTESS *(walking over to the bar):* Can I fix you a drink?

GUEST: You sure can. How about a little vodka and orange juice?

HOSTESS: Coming right up.

GUEST *(surveying the room):* Looks like a nice crowd. I don't think I know anyone here.

HOSTESS: That's no problem. I'll introduce you to several people just as soon as I finish mixing your drink. (Looking directly at the guest) I've been meaning to ask you something since you walked in. From the outline your underwear makes on the seat of your pants, it looks like you're wearing the skimpy, bikini type that clings. Are you?

GUEST *(visibly surprised):* Would you mind running that by me again?

Were you also surprised with the last few lines? Sure you were. Since you know that party script very well—the proper language and demeanor of hostess and guest—the final exchange must have seemed a bit strange. What's even more interesting, however, is that you knew it did not belong in this encounter.

Like a dramatic production, all human interaction is scripted. That is, each communicator has a part (hostess and guest) with lines appropriate for the setting (party). As in theater, we learn our lines during rehearsals, the childhood harnessing period discussed earlier. And when an individual deviates from the script—"Do you wear bikini underwear?"—the actors (communicators) are frequently unable to respond and the production (encounter) suffers.

Each communication encounter, then, is like a one-act play. The props have to be right (sofa, bar, and stereo); the lighting and mood must be appropriate (jazz/rock music and partially lit apartment); and the actors' costumes (jeans, halter tops, and patterned shirts) must be carefully selected. Of course, each play is written and produced by the culture—the source of all situational proprieties—and directed by the actors' parents and peers, the teachers of appropriate communication behavior.

THE POLITICS OF THE COMMUNICATION SYSTEM

Beginning to feel that communication is more structured and controlled than you ever thought? Then this chapter has not been written in vain. As regimented and punitive as any political system, the communication establishment also places behavioral demands on individuals. Failure to conform to communication expectations, be they cultural, regional, or situational, may result in interpersonal misunderstandings, even social ostracism.

Still, every communication system has its revolutionaries who deviate from accepted patterns of interaction. Yearning to be spontaneous, to say and do what they please, these revolutionaries attempt to shake off the communication harness. Their efforts are usually futile, the goal unreachable. Psychological pain and nervous affectation are often their rewards.

Another Revolutionary Bites the Dust

Brad is twenty-nine years old and in serious psychological trouble. A firm believer in authenticity, Brad said and did what he felt which frequently violated communication expectations. He often spoke too loudly in libraries, disclosed too much to strangers, and refused to fabricate excuses to close a conversation. Unwilling to play the part of the servile employee, he was usually fired for his "outspoken" remarks. Convinced the courtship script was also a farce, he normally expressed his feelings very early in a relationship and was usually rejected. Now at age twenty-nine, without a meaningful job and stable emotional relationship, Brad feels his life has been wasted.

Like any political order, the communication establishment maintains stability through a system of rewards and punishments. Individuals who obey the linguistic and behavioral rules of each setting are supported and accepted by those with whom they communicate. People like Brad who challenge the system, defying its communication rules and customs, frequently experience rejection. While in the political order social ostracism is accomplished by jailing the offender, the communication system simply ignores its deviants, with loneliness and alienation serving as a prison.

If you feel the preceding is a bit melodramatic, please reflect on the last time you communicated with someone who breached the communication script. Remember the "rude" waitress, the one who refused to assume the role of the friendly, tolerant, fawning servant? And then there was the stranger on the bus who disclosed very personal information instead of talking about the weather or some other light topic. In both cases, you were uncomfortable, nervous, even angry. Because they violated the proprieties of each setting, you could not wait to escape their presence.

Each of us, then, helps police the communication system, making sure individuals conform to its rules, disciplining those who deviate. We willingly play this role because the system does more than restrict us; it provides security, adding predictability to each communication encounter.

If There Were No Rules

Imagine living in a culture where there were no communication scripts, where individuals could express their innermost feelings whenever they desired. Free to choose your language, how would you interact at a funeral, wedding, or fraternity Christmas party? Similarly, what would others say to you in these social settings; would it be supportive, embarrassing, anxiety producing? Groping for words, unable to predict the responses of others, your anxieties would certainly increase, possibly preventing you from freely interacting.

Evidently, situational proprieties also play a positive role in communication. Not only do they help us select our language and behavior, but they provide us with some assurance that we will not be embarrassed or verbally abused by others. Able to anticipate with some accuracy our own communication and also that of others, we can interact with greater ease.

FINALE: A HAIRCUT

Like a meticulously styled haircut, the way we communicate has been shaped by social context. The primary stylist is culture, carefully trimming our language and behavior to the specifications of the communication system. The grooming is done by one's ethnic group, social class, and regional location, producing a communication style that compliments each individual's background. Finally, situational proprieties—the stylist's hairspray—keep the coiffure in place, making sure our words and movements are appropriate for the social setting.

SUMMARY

1. Verbal and nonverbal communication are learned behaviors, acquired from our culture, social class, ethnic group, and regional location.

   Our language and bodily movements are influenced by many social contexts. Individuals reared in diverse environments often have difficulty communicating with one another.

2. Culture is the foundation of human interaction, influencing our every word and movement.

   Each society has its own communication patterns transmitted from generation to generation. Learned at an early age, these patterns provide a foundation for interpersonal communication.

3. The meaning of words and actions within each society is largely determined by cultural values.

   Commonly called values, each society has certain preferences concerning the way human beings ought to behave. These cultural values not only guide our selection of words and actions, but we use them to interpret the communication of others.

4. Individuals raised in societies with different cultural values frequently misunderstand one another when communicating.

Apparently, value differences in such areas as formalism, role behavior, status, and emotionality have resulted in diverse communication patterns in Italy, America, and Iraq.

5. Interpersonal communication is regulated by contextual rules called situational proprieties.

Situational proprieties determine the verbal and nonverbal communication appropriate for each social setting. Violation of these rules often results in interpersonal misunderstandings, even conflict.

6. The communication system is as structured and ordered as a political system.

Like any political order, the communication system maintains stability through a system of rewards and punishments. Those who obey the linguistic and behavioral rules are supported; individuals who deviate frequently experience rejection.

PRACTICE CASE STUDY

There was nothing unusual about this Saturday night. After seeing a Bergman movie, my wife and I went to a nearby pancake house for a snack. Everything was fine until we ran into Neil, an old friend of ours, at the restaurant.

"Hi Neil, long time no see. How have you and Gloria been?" I queried.

"Didn't you know my wife and I were divorced last month?" he sadly responded.

Unaware of his marital problems, we listened intently while Neil disclosed the unfortunate turn of events. Still talking when the hostess was ready to seat us, I invited Neil to our table.

As we walked to the table, Neil scanned the restaurant as though in search of somebody. Nearing the destination, he suddenly asked the hostess whether we could sit at another table, preferably the one in the corner of the room near a table of young, unescorted females. Instantly I realized what he was looking for.

"Boy, I'd like to meet the brunette sitting at that table," Neil commented. "But how the hell am I going to do that in this restaurant?"

"Why just get up, walk over, and introduce yourself," I naively responded.

"But I can't do that," he answered anxiously. "This place isn't a singles' bar; it's a pancake house."

"Ah, just go on over there and don't come back without a phone number," I remarked playfully.

Off he went.

We watched closely as he approached the women's table, introducing himself to what appeared to be three shocked individuals. Unsure how to react to him, the females stared curiously at Neil while he vainly tried to start a conversation. After a long awkward silence, it was clear Neil was not going to achieve his goal. Excusing himself, he returned to our table, seemingly embarrassed by the incident.

EXPLORATORY QUESTIONS

1. Why do you think I experienced tension when Neil abruptly disclosed that he was recently divorced?

2. Why was Neil so reluctant to introduce himself to the unfamiliar females?

3. Referring to the discussion on communication scripts and situational proprieties, examine Neil's observation that "This isn't a singles' bar; it's a pancake house."

4. Do you think situational proprieties had anything to do with the cold response Neil received from the women? Explain.

5. Why do you think Neil was so nervous before and after his transaction with the women? Was this due to situational proprieties?

6. Did Neil violate any American values when he attempted to meet the unescorted females in the restaurant?

7. Examine my dialogue in terms of the male communication script, particularly the admonition, "Don't come back without a phone number."

8. Did Neil's embarrassment stem from his inability to fulfill masculine expectations with respect to seduction?

ADDITIONAL PROJECTS

1. Conceivably, Neil could have met these females without upsetting them. Rewrite the preceding case so that Neil's communication is a bit more appropriate.

2. What situational proprieties in the restaurant would have to be altered to legitimize Neil's behavior?

INTERPERSONAL COMMUNICATION EXERCISES

1. Situational Propriety Exercise
Would you like to find out how structured and ritualized communication is? Try this exercise.
   A. During your next conversation with a stranger or acquaintance, do the following:
      1. Do not begin the conversation with a perfunctory greeting; just start talking.
      2. Instead of discussing a superficial topic, disclose personal information about yourself.
      3. Dominate the conversation; interrupt your partner. Do not abide by turn-taking rules.
      4. Do not terminate the encounter formally; just walk away.
   B. After informing the subject(s) that this was an experiment, ask the individual to evaluate your behavior.

2. Cultural Values and Communication: An Exercise
To discover how cultural values influence the way we interpret verbal and nonverbal stimuli, participate in the following exercise.
   A. Ask someone to react to these hypothetical situations.
      1. (male interviewee) You have just met a female in a singles' bar. After talking for only a few minutes, she suddenly asks you for your phone number and inquires whether you would like to go out with her next Saturday night.
      2. You have been invited to a friend's house for dinner. Upon entering, you find him arguing with his ten-year-old son who appears to be bawling out his father. In fact, the kid sternly proclaims that his father has "disobeyed him once too often" and must spend the rest of the day in his room.
   B. How did American cultural values associated with gender and age influence the interviewees responses?

3. An Exercise on Context and Communication
How and when do young children learn situational proprieties? Let's find out.
   A. Answer the following questions by interviewing parents and observing young children.
      1. How do parents teach their children to say hello and goodbye? At what age does the child begin conforming to this communication rule?
      2. What methods do parents use to familiarize the child with appropriate eye contact behavior? When does the child first realize that staring is situationally inappropriate?

3. What methods do parents use to teach their kids how to start a conversation? At what age does the child begin initiating conversations appropriately?

NOTES

[1] Jean Piaget, *The Child's Conception of Movement and Speed* (Boston: Routledge & Kegan Paul, 1970); Ray Birdwhistell, *Introduction to Kinesics* University of Louisville, 1952).

[2] Robert Shuter, "A Field Study of Nonverbal Communication in Germany, Italy, and the United States," *Communication Monographs*, vol. 44 (1977), pp. 298–306.

[3] John Condon and Fathi Yousef, *An Introduction to Intercultural Communication* (New York: Bobbs-Merrill, 1975).

[4] Erving Goffman, *Behavior in Public Places* (Glencoe, Il.: Free Press, 1963).

CHAPTER 9

Signifyin' and Stylin' Out:
Subculture and Communication

Transport yourself for a moment to these scenarios. While I am not a mind reader, I am reasonably certain the following is an accurate description of each one of you.

Scenario I

It is the first day of school in any city or town in the United States. Along with thousands of white middle class learners, you are being bused to a school located in the black ghetto. Except for a few "Negroes" that work in your lily white neighborhood and those who appear on television, this will be your first direct experience with black people and culture.

Passing through the ghetto, a section of town you have only seen from behind a closed car window, your anxieties surface.

"Their language is so different: how will I talk to them? Will they hurt me, try to beat me up because I am white? I'm really afraid of them."

Scenario II

You recently accepted a scholarship to attend a predominantly white university in the North. Reared in a black ghetto in Detroit, you have had little contact with the "man" save a few fleeting encounters with store owners, employers, and the like. Because much of your knowledge about "crackers" (whites) has come second hand from disenchanted parents, angry peers, and disgruntled relatives—individuals turned off by a white dominated society—your impressions of Caucasians are not favorable. In fact, you think whites are mean and insensitive, incapable of accepting people of color. Bothered by these nagging stereotypes, anticipating hostile treatment from the white university students, you are experiencing serious doubts about having accepted the scholarship.

Have I characterized you incorrectly? Are the feelings and thoughts I identified unlike those you might experience in these situations? I think not! In fact, it is argued in this chapter that such reactions are unavoidable as long as individuals are unfamiliar with subcultures and their unique communication patterns.

THE AMERICAN DREAM GONE ASTRAY

America is an amalgamation of numerous mini-societies called *subcultures*. Characterized by distinct customs and values, each subculture is a blend of the old world and new, with black-Americans, Polish-Americans, and Chinese-Americans, for example, preserving some of the cultural traditions of their ancestors. Because the United States was ostensibly founded on freedom and equality, members of subcultures were promised that they could maintain their ethnic identity while functioning as American citizens. To have Jew and gentile, black and white, Pole and German respect one another and work together in the creation of a great country was the American dream. Somehow this dream remains an illusion.

Instead, we have built walls between subcultures in the form of ghettos and ethnic neighborhoods. Reared primarily with those of the same subculture, we have had amazingly little contact with many ethnic groups. Having little firsthand information about these groups, we have developed stereotypes to help us understand and interact with subcultural members. Defined as inaccurate generalizations about a group of individuals, stereotypes provide spurious information upon which to make interpersonal judgments; accordingly, they cripple rather than improve communication.

A WALK DOWN STEREOTYPE LANE

Remember as a child when you heard your father use the word *kike* for the first time?

"With inflation eating away at my paycheck, you'd think that boss of mine would have given me a bigger raise. Boy, that guy is a real kike—cheap as they come. He also has a big Jewish mouth, always promising us the world but never coming through. You just can't trust those people; they're always wheeling and dealing."

And then there was the white dentist who your mother complained about for supposedly overcharging her. That was your first experience with the word *honkey*.

"Man, that guy is just like all the rest of those honkeys, always trying to screw black folks. Here he was telling me that the work wouldn't be expensive and he gives me a bill like this! They're all a bunch of liars and cheats."

In addition to kike and honkey, you were probably also introduced at a very early age to *chink, spic, nigger, polock,* and a host of other subcultural slur terms. As indicated, your parents, who you relied on most for information about the world, often provided the initial exposure to these words. Because mommy and daddy were beyond question, these terms, storehouses for virulent ethnic images, were implanted deep in your psyche.

Clearly, parents are not solely responsible for poisoning childrens' minds with stereotypic terms and images. In addition, peers and other adults contribute greatly to this process. The media—television, film, and print—are also major culprits, frequently presenting nigger, kike, and chink images to their audiences.

Bombarded by stimuli that reinforce stereotypes, individuals find it very difficult to alter or extinguish them. Moreover, these faulty generalizations destroy potential human relationships, producing hostility among those who do not even know one another.

Meeting a Stereotype Face to Face:
Some Communication Problems

Returning to Scenario I, let's follow a white student into school where, for the first time, he encounters a black individual.

After leaving the bus, Stuart, visibly nervous, clutching his books as though afraid of being mugged, proceeded to his homeroom. Discovering he was one of the few whites in the class, he took the only available seat, finding himself next to a black student who glanced at him, said nothing, and then turned away. "I knew these blacks were unfriendly," thought Stuart. "I just hope I don't get into a fight before the day ends."

With the ring of the bell to change classes, Stuart rushed from the room, leaving one of his books on the desk. Noticing the forgotten book, the black student called to Stuart, "Hey man, you with the plaid pants on, hold up. I got something for you." Realizing the request may have been intended for him, Stuart, taking no chances, quickened his pace.

Scurrying through the halls, he imagined what the unknown black caller wanted to bestow upon him: an insult, a clenched fist, maybe even a switchblade in the belly. Again the voice rang out. "Plaidpants, will you slow down and take what's coming to you?"

Certain that he was Mr. Plaidpants, Stuart broke into a run. Dashing into the mens' room, Stuart, panting and perspiring, prayed he had lost his assailant in the crowded hall. However, no sooner had he entered a toilet stall, his intended hideout, when the caller rushed into the bathroom. "Plaidpants, are you nuts?" he bellowed. "Will you take your damn book so I can go to my next class?"

Thoroughly embarrassed, Stuart left the stall, making sure his black classmate saw him flush the toilet. He nervously accepted the book, apologizing profusely for running down the hall which, he claimed, was motivated by an intestinal disorder. "I guess he's one of the good ones," thought Stuart, "though you can't be too careful."

CASE ANALYSIS. This case actually occurred while a public school system was being integrated in the fall of 1977. Though humorous, it demonstrates how stereotypes hinder successful interpersonal communication. For starters, consider their effect on message transmission.

Expecting blacks to be hostile and unfriendly, Stuart's interpretation of his "assailant's" actions was not surprising. A stolen glance, a pregnant pause—behaviors the black classmate first displayed—communicated hostility to Stuart because he expected conflict. Similarly, if friendliness and warmth were anticipated, he would have evaluated these actions more positively. Accordingly, our feelings and attitudes about a subculture, including the stereotypes that inhabit our psyches, greatly affect the evaluation of nonverbal messages.

Stuart's attitudes about blacks were also responsible for the preceding running sequence reminiscent of Mack Sennett's Keystone Cops. Under normal conditions, this white student would have stopped immediately if he thought an unknown caller had something for him. However, since the caller was black, the forgotten book was instantly converted into a weapon, resulting in increased fear and panic. And when Stuart heard the ominous cry "take what's coming to you," which was not intended to be a threat, his anxieties overwhelmed him, producing a full gallop.

Before you condemn Stuart, you should realize that he is no more insensitive or brutal than any one of you. In fact, his distortion of the black caller's messages was not deliberate; it was beyond his control. Like you, he is at the mercy of stereotypes, blinders which narrow the field of vision screening out much of the world. These spurious generalizations shape perception in the same manner as do other attitudes and beliefs: insidiously, unconsciously, and thus without the communicator being aware of it. Stereotypes, then, produce a most virulent form of message distortion, one that defies our immediate detection. People like Stuart will have more success communicating with subcultural members only when their stereotypes are extinguished.

ALTERING STEREOTYPES: EASIER SAID THAN DONE

A critical question still remains: Why do we maintain our stereotypes and continue to distort messages even after meeting a subcultural member who violates our expectations? Why are these attitudes so resistant to change? To answer these questions, let's examine the nature and function of stereotypes.

In two fascinating studies conducted by Andrea Rich and Dennis Ogawa, black communication stereotypes of whites are closely examined.[1] Perusing their research, one is struck by the extensive and contradictory nature of these stereotypes. For example, black-Americans expect whites to be evasive, critical, emotional, concealing, sensitive, rude, conservative, boastful, aggressive, and ostentatious. Certainly, it is paradoxical to expect someone to be emotional and concealing or sensitive and rude; nevertheless, because stereotypes are buried deep in our psyches, we rarely reflect on their contradictory nature.

Moreover, with these contradictory descriptions, almost any behavior displayed by a subcultural member can be considered stereotypic. For instance, if a Caucasian is quiet and ambiguous, a black person can charge the individual with being typically "evasive," while a loud, talkative Anglo may be considered an "aggressive and boastful" honkey. Since all of our stereotypes are so easily reinforced, it is no wonder they remain intact, unaltered by direct experience or the passage of time.

However, there comes a time when we encounter an individual who defies labels, one who displays behavior unlike that expected of an ethnic group. As in Stuart's case, rather than alter the stereotype, we often consider that person unrepresentative of the subculture ("I guess he's one of the good ones."). If this does not work, we simply disregard the individual and the behavior, another example of selective perception discussed in Chapter 3. In either case, we have protected our stereotypes; but why guard them so jealously?

The Function of Stereotypes

United Press Release: June 14, 1994

A new mind-altering drug that instantly extinguishes stereotypes has been discovered by a medical researcher in Cleveland, Ohio. Says Dr.

Schmidt about his wonder substance, "Individuals first experience a euphoric feeling after taking the drug and then become acutely depressed. Panic and suicide frequently occur." The Federal Trade Commission is considering Boston and Birmingham as test markets.

As inferred in the preceding press release, stereotypes play a positive function in our lives despite their obvious deficiencies. Without them, we would be unable to sort humanity into simple ethnic bundles. For example, *all* blacks could no longer be considered lazy, and stereotypes about Mexicans would be shattered. Setting aside our collective images, individuals would have to be evaluated on their own merits, a desirable though tension-producing alternative.

So in spite of what you may have thought, you would probably experience a psychological crisis if all your stereotypes were eliminated tomorrow morning. Unable to label others and anticipate their behavior, the world would certainly appear more chaotic. Though inaccurate and oftentimes vicious, stereotypes help us structure reality, bringing order to the "blooming, buzzing, confusion."

Like an individual with whom we are deeply involved, it is difficult to live with stereotypes and disturbing to be without them. However, the psychological pain experienced while divorcing oneself from stereotypes is a small price to pay to see people as they are and communicate successfully with them.

Having looked at stereotypes, let's find out what subcultural members are really like by examining the way they communicate.

PENETRATING STEREOTYPES:
SUBCULTURE AND COMMUNICATION

If you have ever watched members of a subculture interact, you may have noticed that they have their own communication style. That is, their language, body movements, even eye contact patterns may have seemed different than those of most Americans. In trying to discover what these unfamiliar words and actions meant, you probably misinterpreted them on many occasions. These communication idiosyncracies are frequently the cause of interpersonal misunderstandings; accordingly, the following section examines subcultural differences in communication.

SUBCULTURAL ARGOTS

Torn from your family, forced with others to board a slave ship to an unknown destination, you find yourself in an alien society. Stripped of your African culture and language, denied human rights, compelled to live in wretched conditions, physical and psychological survival become paramount concerns.

To stay alive in this hostile environment, you must be able to communicate with members of your group without being understood by the oppressor. So an argot is developed—a secret language shared by members of your group—to get around the "man." With a common code, ethnic pride and group identity are partially restored. As a result, your people are tighter, more cohesive, able to converse without fear of reprisal from the dominant culture.

Subcultures in the United States developed argots for reasons similar to those of black culture. That is, placed in a society unlike their native culture, individuals needed a sublanguage to reaffirm group identity and protect the subculture from unknown exploiters. In fact, Mauer indicates that unless a subculture feels threatened by the larger society, a fully developed argot will not evolve.[2] Similarly, when the subculture is more accepted and the perceived threat diminishes, the argot alters substantially and is frequently adopted by members of the larger society.

Many subcultures, then, have their own language patterns. Unsurprisingly, problems often arise when an individual communicates with a member of a subculture and is unfamiliar with that person's argot. Consider.

Doing the Dozens:
A Look at Black Speech

Jim was raised in lily white Fond du Lac, Wisconsin. Having lived and attended school with whites his entire life, he decided, at age nineteen, to find out what black people were really like. So while attending the University of Wisconsin, he volunteered to be an exchange student for one year at an all-black college in the heart of Mississippi. Though Jim has many vivid recollections of this experience, one moment stands out as the most confusing and tension producing.

Studying in his room one evening, Jim, who had only been at the school for two weeks, was interrupted by a knock at the door. He quickly discovered the caller was LeRoy, his black roommate's friend. Making himself at home, LeRoy indicated that Jesse, Jim's roommate, would be arriving shortly and he wanted to wait for him. So Jim returned to his books, and LeRoy read the newspaper.

Soon afterwards, Jesse entered the room. Seeing LeRoy on the couch, he appeared enraged, attacking Jim for permitting his friend to remain in their quarters. "You dumb honkey!" Jesse screamed. "Why did you let black slick head into the room; don't you know better?"

Startled and puzzled by this unwarranted attack, Jim was about to respond when LeRoy broke in. "Hey nigger, who you calling slick head? If a dog hadn't beat me to your back door, I would have been your daddy."

Turning to LeRoy, Jesse, sober and pensive, quickly responded. "Nappy, I saw your mother layin' in the gutter. I took a piece of glass and stuck it up her ass. I never saw a motherfucker run so fast."

Stunned by the exchange, Jim, mouth opened wide, stared at the two. Fearing physical violence, he thought of interceding but was too scared to move. Instead, he buried his pale white face in his book, hoping they would settle their differences without killing each other.

The room was still. LeRoy, putting both hands in his pockets, glared at Jesse, turned away, then again looked him directly in the eyes. "Is this the bloody finale?" thought Jim. "Should I get out of here before someone jumps on me?" Paralyzed with fear, Jim was frozen to his chair.

"Look, you oreo, you slimy nigger," screamed LeRoy, "give me some skin!" Stretching out his hand, Jesse, smiling broadly, willingly accepted the gentle slap to his palm and then returned the gesture enthusiastically.

Taken aback by the strange turn of events, Jim queried, "You mean you guys were only joking? Aren't you angry with each other?"

"Can you dig it?" responded Jesse. "I couldn't get mad at this nigger; he's too stupid." They were at it again.

CASE ANALYSIS. Called "dozens" in New York, "signifying" in Chicago, "screaming" in Harrisburg, and "chopping" on the West Coast, the preceding exchange of ritualized insults can be an awesome experience for unsuspecting whites. An integral part of black language, the dozens is a verbal game

". . . in which the players strive to bury one another with vituperation. In the play, the opponent's mother is especially slandered . . . Then, in turn, fathers are identified as queer and syphilitic. Sisters are whores, brothers are defective, cousins are funny, and the opponent is himself diseased."[3]

Naturally, those unfamiliar with it might mistake the dozens for a hostile encounter when, in reality, it is a harmless game during which friends test one another's verbal ability.

Learned on the streets at an early age, dozens training begins with memorizing insulting one liners such as "Your mother is so poor she steals care packages" or "Your house is so small roaches walk in single file." In time, the participants learn to create their own put-downs while playing the dozens. Because verbal ability is regarded highly in the black community, the most skillful players are well respected. Some individuals, like Redd Fox and Dick Gregory, convert their chopping talents into a comedy career.

Seemingly an expression of hostility and anger, the verbal exchange in the preceding case was actually a sign of friendship. It was because LeRoy and Jesse were close friends that they could freely "sound out" each other and, at the same time, appreciate the skill and creativity each displayed while playing the game. However, since Jim was a stranger to black culture, he incorrectly assumed that his friends were berating each other. It was not until Jesse and LeRoy abruptly ended their encounter with an affectionate gesture that Jim realized he had witnessed a stylized put-on, a tongue-in-cheek form of verbal combat.

Some individuals refuse to accept chopping as simply a linguistic idiosyncracy of black culture. Convinced that black people are uncivilized, they feel that the dozens demonstrates once again that "Blacks are savages; look how they curse their mothers!" Shucking, jiving, and rapping—additional aspects of black speech—create similar misunderstandings.

Shucking and Jiving with Shirley Temple

The year is 1935, a successful one for Shirley Temple. She has just starred in several movies in which blacks are again portrayed as naive children, eternally grateful to her for protecting them. Seemingly lazy and unintelligent, Miss Shirley's "colored" servants shuffled through her movies with only one concern—pleasing their "massa." When they finally met Miss Dimples, presumably the greatest experience of their lives, the slaves were overwhelmed with excitement, unable to address her without giggling or stammering. Embarrassed, eyes cast down, a poor slave dressed in tattered clothing often expressed the feelings of the group.

"Miss Shirley, I sure hope you likes us. We loves you. You done the best for us. Please be our massa forever." Shirley usually replied, "Because I really like ya'll, I'm going to give each one of you a big piece of my birthday cake."

The slaves appeared so taken by her benevolence that they collectively said the same thing, "Oh thank you Miss Shirley; you so kind." And then ran off to their dilapidated dwellings, laughing uncontrollably.

If the camera had followed the slaves back to their shanties, we would have discovered that the laughter was not prompted by the gift but rather their success at manipulating whitey. That is, the servants had shucked and jived—masking feelings of discontent and frustration with childishness and obedience—until Miss Shirley provided them with additional goods and services.

A product of the South where blacks were constantly reminded "to keep their place," shucking and jiving was used for self-preservation. Realizing that white folks expected and demanded that they appear servile and ignorant, blacks frequently hid their real feelings and thoughts to avoid psychological and physical harm. Though the threat of physical retaliation has diminished, shucking and jiving is still widely used among blacks to secure goods from the "man."

Unfamiliar with shucking and jiving, whites frequently mistake the shuffling, patronizing, confused veneer for the personality of the black communicator. Though the black person's efforts are frequently rewarded with needed goods, this language strategy creates communication problems. That is, compelled to communicate from behind a mask, blacks may be reluctant to express genuine thoughts and feelings to unfamiliar whites. Certainly, this puts a strain on any black/white encounter, severely limiting its potential effectiveness. It appears that the transracial relationship will be marked by continued shucking and jiving until black people have achieved substantial power in American society.

Rapping: A Stylized Narrative

Consider this seduction monologue.

"Hey baby, remember me? I'm the coolest dude you ever met. I'm the ideal man—hip, beautiful, and oh so sexy. I know you can't keep your hands off me, you foxy lady. How about stepping out with me tonight?"

If the preceding was used to seduce a white female, she would have probably laughed hysterically after concluding the speaker was drunk or on the world's longest ego trip. Had the speaker been white her analysis would have probably been accurate. However, since the monologue was presented by a black male, his courtship behavior was most appropriate. He was just "rapping" to a lady.

Rapping is a colorful, imaginative style of communicating marked by lively stories, glib remarks, and frequent references to one's positive attributes. Like the dozens, it is a creative endeavor during which an individual demonstrates verbal skill through storytelling and/or seduction rhetoric. Rapping among black females is also common both in terms of descriptive narrative and "capping" (topping) a male seducer's rap.

> BLACK MALE: Baby, you are the foxiest lady I have ever seen in my life!
>
> BLACK FEMALE: Honey, I'm like a precious gem in a jewelry store. You can look at me but you ain't never going to touch!

Rapping, then, is an expressive way of conveying information characterized by much personal style.

Like other aspects of black argot, rapping is often misunderstood by whites. Overhearing the lively repartee of black seduction, some Caucasians have concluded that these men and women harbor hostile feelings for one another. Similarly, whites frequently watch in amazement as a black narrator of a story prances around the room, gesturing wildly, dropping one descriptive adjective after another. In fact, when conversing with black individuals, whites are sometimes upset, even angered, by their penchant for describing every aspect of an experience. Unaware of the role of storytelling in black culture, whites may even conclude that black people are egomaniacs.

Finale: Language and Subculture

Over the centuries, blacks developed their own language which differed substantially from that of the dominant culture. In addition to blacks, other subcultures also created their own argots. Jews, for example, invented Yiddish—a combination of German, French, and Polish—to communicate with one another. Similarly, Puerto Rican-Americans developed an unusual subcultural argot which consists of a strange blend of Spanish and English.

Complete with its own words, meanings, even grammatical rules, an argot is often misunderstood by those outside the subculture. Only by familiarizing oneself with these language differences can misunderstandings be diminished and conflicts reduced.

NONVERBAL COMMUNICATION: SUBCULTURAL DIFFERENCES

In addition to unique language behavior, subcultures also have distinctive nonverbal communication patterns. Everything from gestures and facial expressions to eye contact and pausing are influenced by subculture. A potpourri of nonverbal idiosyncracies of several subcultures, the following section examines Mexican-Americans, Italian-Americans, black-Americans, and Jewish-Americans.

Time to Burn

You have invited both black and white guests to attend your party. Promptly at nine P.M., the time indicated on the invitation, people begin arriving. By ten o'clock the party still looks like a field of cotton for not a black is in sight.

Several minutes after eleven the first group of blacks finally arrive, followed by a few more at eleven-twenty, and the remaining portion about midnight. Behaving as though they have done nothing wrong, the new arrivals quickly take part in the festivities, never excusing themselves for being late.

How would you have reacted to these late guests? If you are white and unfamiliar with the way black people relate to time, you would have been confused and angry. It would have been simply unforgivable for your guests not to excuse themselves after violating the permissible late period for social events, about one hour in the white world. You might have also interpreted their tardiness as a planned conspiracy to ruin your party or a sign of disrespect and hostility. Moreover, the event could have been twisted to confirm racial stereotypes: "Should I have expected more from these lazy, insensitive people?" However, these interpretations could be no farther from the truth.

Operating on Afro-peoples' time, a hang loose ethic that emphasizes "performing well rather than performing on time," your black guests were not tardy out of disrespect.[4] On the contrary, it was meant as a positive gesture, for it provided the host with additional preparation time; moreover, the guests had time to engage in festivities before coming to the party. In addition, because black parties frequently last until early morning, individuals usually arrive after midnight when things are rolling and people are "mellow." In terms of black standards, then, these guests were not late; they were on time, ready to boogey until dawn.

Additional subcultures in the United States also experience communication problems because their time conception differs radically from that of the larger society. The carefree time orientation of the American Indian, for example, is often construed as laziness and irresponsibility by white employers, frequently resulting in job dismissal. Similarly, the Latin-American penchant for leisurely reflection has been converted in this country into a widely accepted stereotype that Latinos are unwilling to work. Certainly, time often speaks louder than words, particularly when the rigid, inflexible time standard of America is confronted by a hang loose ethic.

Seeing Is Believing

Like many mornings at public school 154 in New York City, a student's wallet has been stolen. This time the theft occurred in a class taught by Miss Krecham, an Irish Catholic from a suburban New York community. After questioning her pupils, all of whom denied committing the theft, she settled on Juan, a fifteen-year-old Puerto Rican student, as her prime suspect. "It's got to be him," she explained to a colleague. "Not only does he sit next to the kid who was victimized, but he won't look me in the eye when I question him."

Accusing a student of a crime for failing to look a teacher in the eye may seem strange, but it actually happened. In fact, several days after Juan's suspension from school, it was discovered that another student in the class had stolen the wallet. However, do not judge Miss Krecham too harshly for you probably would have reached the same conclusion.

Reared in a culture that equates direct eye contact with truthfulness and sincerity, it is no wonder she thought Juan's indirect gaze was an admission of guilt. That is, because Juan refused to look Miss Krecham directly in the eyes, she naturally assumed he was hiding something. What she did not realize, however, was that his behavior was a sign of respect not guilt.

Among Puerto Rican-Americans, gazing directly into an authority figure's eyes is considered insolent and disrespectful. Having acquired his eye contact patterns from this Latin subculture, Juan automatically cast his eyes to the floor when addressed by Miss Krecham, a respected elder. To complicate matters, the Puerto Rican subculture is one of many such groups that have unique eye contact patterns.

For example, if you are white, consider the last time you spoke to a black person. Did the individual's eyes stray from you too often? Did he/she seem more interested in examining the setting than listening to what you were saying? And if you are black, did it appear that the last white person you communicated with tended to stare at you when listening, making the encounter an uncomfortable one? Having had these experiences, you can better appreciate LaFrance and Mayo's findings about black/white differences in eye contact.[5]

They discovered that during a two-person conversation whites tend to look more at the other communicator when listening than when speaking. Blacks, however, were found to engage in more eye contact with their partner when speaking than when listening. With this in mind, it is not surprising that whites are often offended by the black listener's "wandering" eyes. Similarly, it is understandable why blacks are embarrassed, even angered, by the "staring" white listener. Both reactions, however, can be avoided if communicators become familiar with the eye contact patterns of the other races.

In sum, ethnic variations in eye contact can create serious communication problems. Moreover, such problems become increasingly more complex when the communicators differ substantially in a number of nonverbal areas. Consider the following.

Heinz Fifty-Seven: A Potpourri of Nonverbal Communication Differences

Imagine conversing with a male who persists in standing one and a half feet from your nose, about two feet closer than you normally interact. In addition to invading your personal zone, a topic discussed in Chapter 5, this individual cannot seem to keep his hands to himself, frequently attempting to touch, hold, or embrace you. Constantly using exaggerated hand and arm movements to animate his message, he also gestures wildly.

Because middle class white Americans are generally noncontact oriented, upset by those who either stand too close or are too tactile, you would probably consider this individual exceedingly strange. You might even interpret his nonverbal behavior as a sign of criminality, homosexuality, or emotional disturbance. Feeling terribly uncomfortable, you would probably attempt to increase the distance between you and your partner, positioning your body so that his touch could be easily avoided.

Reared in a contact subculture where touching, close conversational distance, and expressive gestures are encouraged, your partner was certainly neither homosexual nor disturbed; he was a Mexican-American. In fact, Mexicans often consider Anglo-Americans to be cold, unfriendly, and aloof because they refuse to engage in much contact and prefer conversing at three and a half feet or more. Unsurprisingly, problems arise when a Chicano converses with a white middle class American to whom touching and close conversational distance are signs of intimacy.

Apparently, the Mexican-American penchant for contact and dramatic gestures is shared by several other subcultures in the United States. Jewish-Americans, for example, are reported to be very tactile, with adult males, particularly a father and son, frequently embracing each other in public.[6] Like Jews, Italian-Americans are supposed to be notorious touchers, and they also interact at a closer distance than do most middle class white Americans.[7]

However, when it comes to unusual nonverbal behavior, particularly in terms of gesture and body posture, black America wins hands down. For example, giving and getting skin, which consists of palm-

to-palm contact between two black interactants, is often used to convey agreement or approval (above). Similarly, "five on the sly," a knuckle-to-palm contact between two communicators, serves to increase rapport and heighten intimacy (page 150).

In terms of body posture, black men and women have very distinctive styles. The male "peeping" stance, marked by a dipped right shoulder, hands deep in trouser pockets, is for girl watching, especially when "digging a woman's action" (observing her hips roll) (page 151). "Woofing," a pose assumed by both black men and women (page 152), is used while bragging or boasting. Finally, the "rapping" stance, characterized by frequent gestures and intimate distancing, is usually employed by a black male when seducing a woman (page 153). Naturally, whites unfamiliar with nonverbal behavior in black culture may misinterpret these gestures and postures, and attach meanings not intended to be conveyed.

STEREOTYPES AND BEYOND

Now do you see why it is easier to live with stereotypic images of a subculture than experience the people behind them? Venturing

beyond our stereotypes, we often find a complex of verbal and non-verbal behaviors that seemingly defy our understanding. Rather than determine the significance of these unfamiliar behaviors, it is much easier to dismiss them as the peculiarities of a strange subculture. Accordingly, genuine understanding of a subcultural group requires knowledge and effort, an investment too few are willing to make.

Sickness or Health: A Concluding Statement

Like cancer cells, stereotypes are not easily extinguished. In fact, they often multiply in number, altering and distorting the very substance of interpersonal communication—our perceptions. Unless individuals are exposed to accurate information, the only known treatment for diseased ideas, they will deteriorate communicatively, unable to converse effectively with subcultural members. To fully recover, we must commit ourselves to understanding each subculture's life experiences and communication patterns, thus opening each of us to meaningful new relationships.

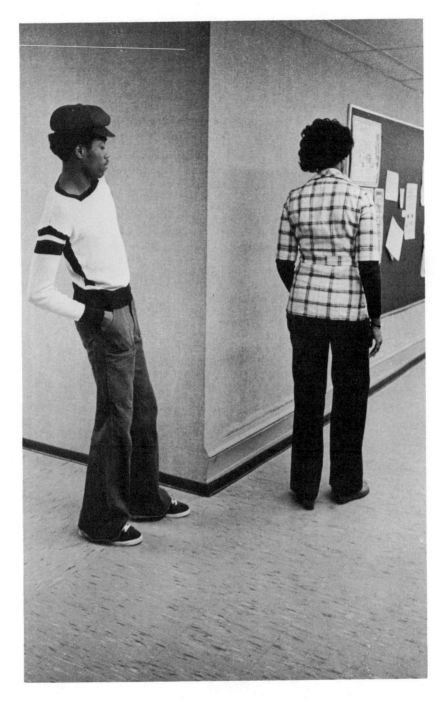

SUMMARY

1. Stereotypes cripple interpersonal communication.

   Individuals often rely on stereotypes when communicating with subcultural members. However, because stereotypes provide spurious information upon which to make interpersonal judgments, they can destroy potential encounters.

2. Stereotypes are learned at an early age from parents, peers, and the media.

   Reared in a culture replete with subcultural stereotypes, it is not surprising that by age five many of these faulty generalizations are internalized. Reinforced by parents, peers, and the media, these images are indelibly etched in our memory.

3. Stereotypes are difficult to alter.

   Because stereotypes help us sort reality into simple ethnic bundles, they serve a useful function. We protect our stereotypes by seeking out information that confirms them, while dismissing that which is contradictory.

4. Stereotypes unknowingly manipulate our perception, producing message distortions that defy our immediate detection.

   Stereotypes, like all attitudes and beliefs, influence what we see and hear. They serve as a filter through which all information must pass, thus resulting in distorted message reception.

5. Each subculture has its own verbal and nonverbal idiosyncracies which are frequently misunderstood by the larger society.

   For purposes of self-defense and group identification, many subcultures have developed their own language that often differs substantially from the commonly accepted code. Similarly, because nonverbal behavior is also influenced by subculture, it is frequently misunderstood by those unfamiliar with the group.

6. Among others, blacks, Chicanos, Jews, Puerto Rican-Americans, and Italian-Americans have unique communication styles.

   After examining the communication patterns of these subcultures, it was discovered that they differed from white middle class Americans in such areas as language, eye contact, tactility, gesture, body posture, time orientation, and conversational distance.

PRACTICE CASE STUDY

It was summertime and Annette, a sophomore at a state university, was in desperate need of money. Eager to earn enough for next year's tuition, she finally landed a job in a factory after weeks of unsuccessful interviews. While the salary was adequate for a temporary position, she was troubled by the working conditions, particularly the individuals with whom she must toil.

Hired as an unskilled laborer, Annette was supposed to function as an assembly line worker in a factory composed primarily of lower class whites. A black woman raised in a Chicago ghetto, Annette was afraid the other workers might verbally or physically abuse her. If her monetary needs were not so great, she never would have shown up the first day of work.

Arriving twenty minutes early that day, she approached the employee window to pick up her punch card. While asking for it, she noticed a few white office workers staring strangely at her. Annette immediately reacted, "Hey girls, haven't you ever seen a black woman before?" Surprised by Annette's remark, the women nervously resumed working.

Distressed that a problem would arise so early, Annette walked into the work area, reflecting on whether she ever should have taken the job. While deep in thought, she accidentally walked into a passing factory worker.

"Hey baby," observed Al, the factory's most notorious seducer and comedian, "let's get it on after work, not during."

Expecting a smile and a few friendly words, Al instead received a long stare, followed by a seriously delivered warning that he should "watch his mouth in the future." Too stunned to reply, Al continued on his way, muttering to himself. Annette decided to stay clear of the other laborers by sitting as far from them as possible, speaking only when addressed.

Most of Annette's initial encounters that day were just as disastrous as those previously described. She punched out early and was never seen again.

EXPLORATORY QUESTIONS

1. Identify and examine the various stereotypes Annette may have had about white people.

2. In what ways do you think these stereotypes influenced Annette's demeanor and perception of her co-workers?

3. What effect did Annette's stereotypes have on her interpretation of the messages she received from others?

4. How did these faulty generalizations influence the messages she transmitted to her co-workers?

5. Do you suppose Annette's stereotypes about white people were reinforced by the encounters she had with her co-workers?

6. Why do you think the white personnel clerks stared curiously at Annette?

7. How do you suppose the laborers evaluated Annette's attempt to separate herself from them?

8. Do you think Annette's behavior would have confirmed the stereotypes that the white workers may have had of blacks?

ADDITIONAL PROJECTS

1. If you were manager of this company, how could you resolve this transracial problem? Develop a plan that would minimize message distortion and interpersonal conflict.

2. Having the benefit of hindsight, rewrite the preceding case so that the interactions turn out positively.

INTERPERSONAL COMMUNICATION EXERCISES

1. Stereotyping Exercise
   Stereotypes abound in our culture. To demonstrate this, try this exercise.
   A. Divide the class into small groups. Ask each group to jot down as many adjectives as it can think of that might be associated with the following subcultural members.
      1. Jews
      2. Mexicans
      3. Blacks
      4. Poles
      5. Puerto Ricans
   B. Have each group write its results on the blackboard. As a class, discuss the adjectives, noting the many contradictory impressions.

2. The Function of Stereotypes: An Exercise
   Do stereotypes really help us sort reality into simple ethnic bundles? The following exercise may help you answer this question.
   A. Interview four people, preferably a teenager, college student, middle-aged person, and elderly individual. Ask each interviewee the following questions. Be ready to ask them additional probing questions as well.
      1. In your estimation, what are Jews like?
      2. In your estimation, what are Blacks like?
      3. In your estimation, what are Poles like?
   B. After you have collected your data, bring the information to

class and share your speculations with the others. The class analysis should focus on the varied impressions of each age group and the function of the stereotypes for the interviewees.

3. Subculture and Nonverbal Communication: An Exercise
Many subcultures have their own distance and contact patterns. To find out more about these patterns, participate in this experience.
   A. Divide the class into groups of four to six members. Each group should select a different subculture to research. The groups should also locate several places where members of the chosen subculture can be observed as they communicate.
   B. In conducting your research, examine only two person groups. To the nearest half-foot, estimate the distance at which your subjects interact. Also record the amount of times the communicators touch each other during a two-minute interval. After examining several dyads, compute the average for both distance and tactility.
   C. Bring your results to class and discuss the distance and tactile orientations of the selected subcultures.

NOTES

[1] Andrea Rich, *Interracial Communication* (New York: Harper & Row, 1974) pp. 51–63.

[2] David Mauer, "Linguistic Hostility as a Factor in Intra-Cultural Conflict," *Actes du Dixieme Congrès des Linguistes* (Bucharest: Editions de L'Academie de la République Socialiste de Roumaine, 1969).

[3] Mack McCormick, *The Dirty Dozens: The Unexpurgated Folksongs of Men*, Arhoolie Record Album, 1960.

[4] Arthur Smith, *Transracial Communication* (Englewood Cliffs, N.J.: Prentice-Hall, 1973).

[5] Marianna LaFrance and Clara Mayo, "Gaze Direction in Interracial Dyadic Communication," presented at the Eastern Psychological Assn., Washington, D.C., May, 1973.

[6] Ashley Montagu, *Touching: The Significance of the Skin* (New York: Columbia University Press, 1971).

[7] Robert Shuter, "A Field Study of Nonverbal Communication in Germany, Italy, and the United States," *Communication Monographs*, vol. 44 (1977), pp. 298–306.

CHAPTER 10

Doctor, Lawyer, Indian Chief:
Social Roles and Communication

Set deep in the mountains of northern California overlooking breath-taking gorges and floral life stands Sandstone, a radical experiment in human relationships. A commune founded on liberating people from the restraints of conventional society, Sandstone is committed to revitalizing interpersonal communication.

By requiring members to remove their clothing—symbolically stripping them of societal inhibitions—Sandstone encourages its participants to encounter one another in any way they desire. Sexual and conversational intimacies are freely shared, with single and married members frequently establishing short-lived sexual relationships and/or more enduring unions with one or several people in the commune. Save violence, no form of expression is prohibited; individuals can say and do as they please.

In other words, males and females need not limit their intimate relationships to those of the opposite sex, and husbands and wives can openly develop deep unions with additional people. Moreover, group sex and three-member marriages, affairs of pleasure and those of substance are all sanctioned. In short, Sandstone assaults social roles by permitting men and women, husbands and wives, friends and lovers to communicate with whomever they please and in any way they choose. Unlike conventional institutions, then, Sandstone does not require its members to behave in certain ways just because they happen to assume a particular social role.

To be sure, Sandstone is not unique; in fact, it is only a manifestation of a much wider revolution in this country attempting to free people from sex roles, marital roles, religious roles, and other social roles. However, before one can appreciate this liberation movement, it is first necessary to understand social roles and their impact on language and behavior.

SOCIAL ROLES: INITIAL DIMENSIONS

Within each institution, be it home or office, school or family, all of us play one or more social roles. Members of many institutions, we assume several roles, all of which are most demanding. As daughter or son, mother or father, employer or employee, we are expected to behave in certain ways. Why, the fact that you are pondering my words, internalizing the profundities in this book, is an indication of just how demanding the student role is. Defined in part by one's position in an institution, a social role significantly influences verbal and nonverbal behavior. However, you need not take my word as gospel. Reflect on your own student experiences for verification.

A Mass for Class

Buzzing with activity, the class, anxiously awaiting the arrival of the professor, is alive with intellectual discussions about such deep topics as the upcoming beer party, next weekend's date with fast hands Harold, and Melvin's "good stuff" from Columbia. With the arrival of the professor, the high priest, a hush settles over the congregation.

The students' masks of gaiety and excitement are exchanged for one of pensive reflection. Sitting up in their chairs, slumped bodies stiffen, appearing eager and alert. Eyes focused on the high priest who remains hidden behind the holy shrine, his podium, the congregation awaits the day's sermon.

Carefully arranging his religious artifacts—books, notes, and memoranda—the professor readies himself for the benediction. Dressed in the sect's habit—worn dark blue blazer, faded grey pants three inches too short, and an antique red and white tie—he finally emerges from behind the shrine and announces clearly and soberly that he is a homosexual.

Surprised? Of course you were. Professors are not expected to make that type of disclosure in class. They are also not supposed to curse, use vivid sexual allusions, or dress in a tee shirt, cut-offs, and sandals. For they are priests in their own right and therefore expected to be stoic, formal, and dowdy, a figure worthy of respect. Their speech, body movements, even appearance are well regulated by the professorial role.

Turning to the learners, they rapidly assumed the *student* role with the arrival of the professor. Putting on a mask of deference, passivity, and servility—the expected attributes of students—the class members tailored their behavior to the social role. Serious, formal, and respectful, the students' language also reflected their status. Even their postures changed from a casual pose to a formal one.

Not all students and teachers respond to their social roles in exactly the same ways. Some professors exchange formalism for spontaneity, others trade in their tacky garb for identifiable mod attire. Within limits, then, individuals are free to *enact* their *expected* roles in ways that are compatible with their personalities.

ON LEARNING SOCIAL ROLES

If you think about it, it is amazing that all of us seem to know what type of communication is permissible for each social role. That is, we are quite aware that priests are not supposed to engage in the rhetoric of seduction, obscenities should not be used by parents, and husbands are to refrain from having too much eye contact with other women, especially in the presence of their wives. When and how did we learn these things; who taught us the language and behavior associated with each social role?

Genesis: Pink Booties or Blue?

In the beginning there was freedom. Like all newborn infants, we had no conception of who we were nor did we recognize those we encountered. Our behavior was spontaneous, our reactions genuine. We were free of all social roles.

Then came social conditioning, the culture's primary mechanism for teaching its inhabitants social roles. Through our parents, society's most effective social conditioners, we discovered our first social role: gender.

Remember how embarrassed you were when your mother put you on display while dressed in only a bright new pink diaper with booties to match? Then she took a pink bow that seemed larger than you and taped it to your bald head. Why, you cried for days until she finally realized that your head was not a spliced wire—black electrical tape was not necessary. It was this early association with blue or pink—symbols of maleness and femaleness, respectively—that helped determine your sex role.

In time, you learned what the pink and blue booties really signified. Communicatively, the blue ones required that little boys appear aggressive, competitive, and dominant. Crying was taboo, a romantic overture was "girl stuff," and conspicuous display of love, warmth, or sensitivity was unmanly. With astonishing speed, boys learned what their sex role required of them.

Conversely, the lucky wearers of the pink booties were expected to be "good little girls": passive, nonassertive, emotional, cooperative, respectful, and obedient. They were also taught that it was their duty to accept and support those they encountered, particularly males. Finally, females learned that public display of emotion was sanctioned, and aggressive behavior was unfeminine. Bombarded by these role expectations from birth, it is no wonder we rapidly learned our "genderlects"—male and female communication patterns.

To fully understand social roles, particularly sex roles and gender-linked communication, you should be familiar with the intricacies of role learning. Let's take a closer look.

The Making of a Social Role

Young children are experts at imitating others; in fact, it is their primary mechanism for learning. For example, if you have ever closely watched an infant and parent interact, you may have noticed that the adult's every smile and frown was reflected on the child's face. While you may have dismissed this as cute and insignificant, role theorists like George Herbert Mead argue that this is how social roles are first acquired.[1] That is, in the fundamental stage of role learning, the infant imitates the communicative behavior of others, thus partially enacting several social roles without even being aware of it.

With the passage of time, children take increasingly more roles. Having acquired language, now capable of bringing meaning to the world in which they live, children begin to understand the roles they take. Moreover, they begin discriminating between social roles, assuming those most compatible with their gender. To illustrate this, try to visualize several children playing house.

Why surely you remember the allocation of family roles: Girls become docile mothers and obedient children, while boys assume the roles of dominant father and aggressive sibling. Similarly, violation of family roles is conspicuously evident, with deviant family members immediately corrected by the other children: "Jane, a mommy is supposed to take care of the children. Why don't you?" And because kids are frequently carbon copies of their own parents, those used to being screamed at or hit often display abusive behavior when playing adult roles. Accordingly, role simulations like house and doctor are more than games for they provide children with the opportunity to enact and experiment with a variety of social roles.

In the last stage of role learning, the child assumes social roles symbolically rather than physically. Overwhelmed by many social roles, too old to engage in childish simulations, youngsters no longer imitate the behavior of others. Instead, they *infer* what it is like to be a policeman or teacher, for example, thus dispensing with the physical enactment of these and other social roles. Able to project themselves into the roles of others, children can determine what is expected of them if they assume a particular social role.

Role learning, then, is a complex affair. Nevertheless, we all seem to know the appropriate behavior, demeanor, mask, and costume of each social role.

THE MASQUERADE PARTY: ROLES AND COMMUNICATION

Think of life as an unending masquerade party. Compelled to play many roles, we are constantly changing our costumes and masks. As a white collar worker, you are expected to wear the mask of obedience, respect, and seriousness, while dressed in a J. C. Penney pin-striped suit, white shirt, and tie—the costume of the trade. On arriving home, a quick change of garb and demeanor qualifies you to assume the roles of parent and husband.

Now confident, powerful, and directive—the traditional communication mask of fathers and husbands—you hope to command the respect so often missing at the office. And when it is time to retire, you reveal your most seductive lover costume, put on the mask of tenderness, and emit a few loving words.

Of course, you realize the masquerade party is much larger than this. In fact, each individual changes costumes and masks as many as twenty-five times each day according to Jurgan Ruesch, a noted psychiatrist.[2] With so many roles to assume, we are literally trapped by role expectation, rules that guide our speech and behavior. Since violation of these expectations often results in interpersonal misunderstandings, even conflict, we are reluctant to remove the mask and costume and be ourselves. Consider.

Communication Expectations: Lost, Stolen, or Strayed

Twenty-two years old, brand new college degree in hand, I accepted my first teaching position at a private high school in Chicago. Composed of students who either dropped out or were tossed out of public schools, replete with foreign students from twenty countries and mentally disturbed learners from a nearby institution, the school presented some unusual challenges, particularly for a new teacher. Sustained by the belief that human beings are inherently good, I valiantly entered the learning jungle.

Decked out in my identifiable teaching costume—tweed sport coat, bell-bottom pants, and open, patterned shirt—I opened the classroom door and was greeted by an uproarious tumult. "Will everyone please sit down!" I screamed. To my amazement, the chaos ceased; nevertheless, several students remained standing, all of whom appeared to be foreigners. It was only after the Asians bowed gracefully to me and the Latin Americans extended a formal greeting that they, too, took their seats.

I was about to introduce myself to the class when a burly black student bluntly asked where I bought my clothes. Taken aback by the question, I tried to dismiss it but was encouraged by the rest of the class to answer.

One after another the American kids spoke out without raising their hands, asking a range of questions including whether I was a "mean asshole" like the other teachers in the school. Realizing I had to be flexible, I did not excoriate them for speaking out or using obscenities. In fact, I laughed and joked with the students to establish rapport.

Leaving the sanctuary of the lectern, I also sat with my students and conducted class as though it were a large rap group. Feeling relaxed, I put my feet up on a nearby chair, casually stretching out. While the Americans seemed pleased with the class, the foreign students, particularly the Asians, remained an enigma; they just stared at me without uttering a sound.

The class seemed to be going well until five Asian learners respectfully cornered me one day. The group's spokesman exclaimed.

"Mr. Shuter, we do not think you are acting like a teacher. Why do you permit students to talk out in class and use bad words? We also do not understand why you sit in circle with feet in chair. We think, too, that teacher should be more serious and not joke with student."

Experiencing feelings of anger and frustration, I just stared at the group in disbelief. With only two weeks of teaching under my belt, I could not effectively handle their objections.

After offering them what I knew was an unsatisfactory excuse, they left. Proceeding directly to the principal's office, the students asked to be transferred out of my class. They achieved their goal, and I almost lost my job.

CASE ANALYSIS. Though I felt like wringing the students' necks after they went to the principal, I now understand why they did so. Unknowingly, I caused this communication breakdown; let me explain.

Reared in Cambodia, Thailand, and Vietnam, the five learners were taught that teachers were superior beings, worthy of respect and adoration. In their countries, the instructor was expected to maintain geographical and psychological distance from the students at all times. Always formal and serious in the classroom, the Asian teacher was supposed to command complete obedience from his students.

With these teacher expectations, it is no wonder the Asian learners were dismayed with the way I communicated. Friendly, casual, and open, I behaved much differently than any instructor they had ever experienced. To sit with my students and permit them to speak out in class was considered by the Asians as a sign of weakness and diminished power. Even my nonverbal behavior, a relaxed pose with my feet up on a nearby chair, violated their notion of the formal, serious instructor. In the Asian learners' estimation, I had compromised my integrity by communicating as I did and could no longer be respected.

In addition to the preceding analysis, several important communication principles can be gleaned from the case. First, it clearly demonstrates that misunderstandings may occur when an individual's communication is not compatible with a social role. That is, unable to figure out much of the world in which we live, we would at least like to think that teachers and lawyers, used-car salesmen and politicians will interact in predictable ways. When these expectations are violated, we are frequently surprised, shocked, even angered.

To further illustrate this principle, just imagine what would happen if the President of the United States began the State of the Union Address with a dirty joke. The public would assume the chief of state either collapsed psychologically or had been watching too many X-rated movies. A case of shattered communication expectations, the citizenry would most likely conclude that the person was no longer fit to be President.

The high school case also revealed why people obediently conform to the communication expectations of each social role. Anticipating social censure with each role violation, individuals are reluctant to stray from expected communication patterns. At the job interview, for example, we appear confident, responsible, and pliant, carefully choosing our words and actions no matter how much we dislike the role of interviewee. And while working as a waiter or waitress, we must wear a perpetual smile, serving our customers politely and enthusiastically if a satisfactory tip is desired. We dare not shed our situational masks and costumes for fear of sacrificing potential payoffs.

While there are social rewards for conforming to one's roles—a large tip, a good job, a successful teaching experience—we loose part of ourselves when our public façade is substantially different from our private self. Writes Sidney Jourard, a humanistic psychologist:

> "All too often the roles that a person plays do not do justice to all of his self. In fact, there may be nowhere where he may be himself. He may be self alienated. His real self becomes a feared and distrusted stranger."[3]

To further examine the impact of role expectations on psychological well-being and communicative success, let's look closely at the male sex role.

BROTHER CAN YOU SPARE A TEAR? SEX ROLES AND COMMUNICATION

With the publication of Betty Friedan's *Feminine Mystique*, one of the most influential books of contemporary times, women began to realize that their feelings of self-doubt and powerlessness were shared by other females. Trapped both psychologically and communicatively by their social role, women banded together to bring public attention to their plight. Declaring war on female role expectations, the women's liberation movement indicated that females can have meaningful lives outside marriage and the family, that they need no longer be passive and nonassertive. It was not until much later that groups of men began examining the lethal aspects of the male role.

Born to compete, men are supposed to be achievers, striving for success with the first breath of life. To attain this goal, males are raised to be aggressive and emotionally unexpressive, a potentially successful communication repertoire in a competitive society. For a man to be freely affectionate and tender, to weep publicly during moments of despair and happiness are signs of weakness in many cultures. Though masculine communication patterns are effective in the economic marketplace, they have harmed men psychologically.

Jourard and Lasakow, for example, have shown repeatedly that men disclose much less of themselves than do women.[4] Certainly, men are not devoid of intimate thoughts and feelings, but rather they do not express many of them. Because personal disclosure, particularly a revelation of feelings, leaves one vulnerable, no wonder the competitive male, jockeying for a position in the economic jungle, hides much of his private self from others. Filled with unexpressed feelings, unable to share much of their inner world, males often experience a stress and tension beyond that produced by daily activities. According to some researchers, it is this tension that leads to sickness and early death among males.

In addition to its psychological effects, the male role frequently prevents men from establishing deep human relationships. Moreover, it puts a severe strain on the male/female encounter, often causing a relationship to collapse. Consider.

The Battle of the Sexes

Enduring encounters thrive on reciprocal sharing, where both individuals freely disclose personal thoughts and feelings. An unwillingness by one partner to reveal the private self places an obvious strain on the relationship. In some cases, it relegates the encounter to an impersonal level, preventing the creation of a lasting union. Given the male penchant for secrecy, it is reasonable to assume that men experience more problems than women in developing and sustaining relationships of intimacy. This is demonstrated most dramatically in the heterosexual encounter.

Unlike men, women are encouraged by society to explore and express their feelings. Because of their social conditioning, women reared in the motherhood and wifely tradition learn to value feelings. Apparently, this training results in a positive orientation toward self-disclosure. It is this radical difference in disclosure patterns between men and women that has kept the sexes battling over the centuries. To illustrate this, examine your own relationship for a moment.

When was the last time you wondered why your boyfriend, lover, and/or husband did not express warm, loving feelings more often? Maybe you became so frustrated with his behavior that you brought it up to him and found that he quickly dodged the issue. And males, remember how you resented being pressured to express feelings that you would have rather kept to yourself?

Get the picture? In many relationships, the female is disturbed that her partner is seemingly unwilling to express deep feelings, while the male feels pressured to make what he believes are unnecessary, even threatening disclosures. Hostility and conflict are the by-products of this communication impasse.

Along with being psychologically destructive, traditional sex roles seem to inhibit communication between men and women. To be sure, this is not limited to male/female relationships, for social roles can contaminate any communication encounter.

M & M'S ARE WE: ROLE-TO-ROLE COMMUNICATION

It can be said that each of us is surrounded at all times by a shell within which lives a private self with intimate thoughts and feelings. During our daily transactions, we often forget that behind each "shell"—be it the police officer shell, student shell, or the like— there is a person. In those instances where we cannot or will not penetrate the shell, we are communicating with a social role and thus only superficially touching the person living within.

I Never Sang for My Father

Eighteen years old and away from home for the very first time, Ed, a college freshman, has recently learned while at school that his father left home and was seeking a divorce. Without warning, Ed's life altered radically.

Sad and bitter, he was unable and unwilling to accept his father's decision. "I just don't understand it," observed Ed during a session with his university counselor. "My dad seemed satisfied with his life; he never told me about his problems." Ed realized during the counseling session that his father never disclosed much of anything to him.

Why, Ed knew the individual who took care of his every need, the strong, confident figure who never missed a day at work. He was familiar with the guy who paid the bills, mowed the lawn on Saturday, and bawled out the kids when they were unruly. But Ed never really knew Sam Barns, the person he tenderly called dad. Somehow he missed Sam Barn's private world, his doubts and dilemmas, problems and fears. For eighteen years, Ed had communicated with a *parent* not a *person.*

CASE ANALYSIS. Ed's case is not unique. In fact, family counseling journals report many similar situations where parents and children fail to touch one another as people. That is, they communicate role to role rather than person to person—a case of *role contamination,* a concept first described by Sidney Jourard.[5]

We all know of parents who want their children to succeed so badly that they fail to hear the siblings' anguished cry for independence and freedom. Then there are children who are so busy asking favors of mother that they never once consider how she feels about *her* life and *her* daily responsibilities. Both are examples of role contamination, for the interactants are unable and/or unwilling to communicate with the person behind the social role.

To be sure, role contamination is not limited to family members. In fact, most of our daily encounters are with social roles rather than with people. Have you ever really communicated with the cop on the corner, reached in and discovered what the officer thinks and dreams? And then there is the middle-aged lady who checks out your groceries every Saturday at the supermarket; who is she, what are her fears and desires? How about the postman, sales clerk, telephone operator, nurse, lawyer, and doctor; have you ever interacted with the persons behind these roles? Maybe you have, but only on rare occasions. Why?

Number Please: The Marketplace and Roles

For optimum efficiency and productivity, the marketplace demands that individuals engage in role-to-role communication. Can you imagine what would happen if each passenger boarding the bus at rush hour penetrated the driver's social shell? Why, people would be left on corners throughout the city and the bus would never reach its destination. Similarly, the profits of the telephone company would decline substantially if each of us called an operator and genuinely inquired about her longings and joys.

"Information operator. What number would you like?"

"Operator, I'm not interested in a telephone number. I just want to find out more about you. What makes you tick, your desires and goals."

"I'm sorry, sir. We are not permitted to give out personal information."

"You don't seem to understand, operator. I just read this book about role contamination and am desperately trying to touch another human being."

"I'm sorry sir; have you tried dial-a-prayer?"

Compelled by the economic system to communicate from behind social roles, we hesitate to reveal our real selves for fear of compromising our responsibility to the company and its profits. Moreover, we have been trained so well that those who attempt to penetrate these roles are often considered strange.

A certain degree of role contamination, then, is needed in the marketplace to maintain order and stability. However, if displayed in families and other enduring unions, role contamination can wreak havoc on the relationship, preventing the participants from ever knowing one another. Hence, the trick, according to Franklin Shaw and others, is to avoid as much role contamination as possible by enacting our roles "personally," making them an extension of our private self.[6] In this way, we can partially escape the alienation from self and others described in this section.

However, since the many roles we play make conflicting demands on us, it appears that part of our private self is inevitably compromised whenever we enact a social role. Reflect on the following.

INTERROLE CONFLICT

This case is about Claire, a twenty-six-year-old law school graduate who is having difficulty being a wife, mother, and lawyer. Influenced by the women's movement in college, Claire thought there would be few problems performing all three roles as long as she married an understanding man. As she discovered, it was not as easy as it seemed.

Billy, Claire's husband, readily accepts her involvement in both domestic and legal activities; nevertheless, he is disturbed with the way she communicates at home. For example, while Claire is fulfilling her judicial responsibilities, she is expected to be aggressive and assertive, necessary communication attributes to succeed in the legal marketplace. However, at five o'clock, Billy would like her to replace the mask of dominance with one of tender submissiveness, a style more compatible in his eyes with the roles of wife and mother. Unable to satisfy Billy's domestic expectations, Claire is experiencing a psychological crisis, and the relationship is faltering.

CASE ANALYSIS. Claire's plight is not unusual. Like many professional women, she is at the mercy of conflicting communication expectations. Encouraged to be submissive at home and assertive on the job, Claire is feeling the stress of *interrole conflict*.

To be sure, women are not the only ones trapped by conflicting role demands. Any individual who assumes two or more roles may be placed in a conflict situation. Take former President Gerald Ford, for example.

When his son Jack publicly proclaimed in a pre-election year that he enjoyed smoking marijuana, Gerry was placed in a delicate situation. As President, most citizens expected Ford to take a strong stand against the drug and those who support it. Still, he was Jack's father, obligated to defend and protect his son's reputation. Caught by these conflicting role demands, Ford resorted to evasive ambiguities when asked about Jack's admission.

Needless to say, interrole conflict is not a pleasant experience for it produces psychological and interpersonal tension. Unable to survive for an extended time period under constant stress, relationships experiencing much role conflict often deteriorate slowly or collapse catastrophically. We frequently pay a heavy price for enacting many social roles.

In spite of these difficulties, some social scientists feel that human beings could not function effectively without roles and the attendant communication expectations. Arguing that social roles help us predict the behavior of others, these researchers disapprove of communes and other role-altering experiments. Before examining alternative social roles, let's find out how traditional roles assist us in our daily interactions.

SOCIAL ROLES AND PREDICTABILITY

Enrolled in a public speaking course, Leonard, a freshman at a midwestern university, is about to deliver his first speech. Let's listen to the opening.

"Most of you have probably noticed the adorable fashions men and women are wearing this year. Dear me, I just flip over all the lavenders and aquamarines people are decked out in. Why I haven't seen such divine clothing in years!"

Notice anything strange about the way Leonard is speaking, particularly his choice of subject and words? He is talking like a woman, using adjectives, colors, and discussing a topic normally reserved for females. Leonard has violated the male "genderlect"—a dialect designed for American men—and we all seem to know it. In fact, some of you may have concluded that Leonard was a homosexual just because he used a few "female" phrases.

Peculiar as it may seem, researchers have found that men and women speak different languages. Robin Lakeoff, a noted linguist, has reported that women generally (1) avoid using strong expletives, (2) make finer color discriminations than men, (3) address subjects considered trivial in the real world, (4) and utilize more descriptive adjectives than males. For example, adjectives like adorable, charming, sweet, lovely, and divine are normally for women only. Similarly, such colors as lavender, aquamarine, ecru, and beige are almost strictly used by females, leaving men with the old standards: black, orange, blue, and the like. In explaining these language differences, Lakoff writes:

"Since women are not expected to make decisions on important matters, they are relegated to noncrucial decisions as a sop. Deciding whether to name a color lavender or mauve is one such sop."[7]

Returning to Leonard's speech for a moment, let's discover why you reacted so strongly to the phrase "Dear me." Had Leonard said "shoot," "oh dear," "gosh darn it," or "goodness," you would have been just as surprised. But why?

Expecting men to use strong expletives to express their emotions, you probably considered Leonard's word choice unmasculine. To verify this, ask several people to identify the sex of the following speakers.

Speaker A: "Oh dear, you've let the dog in the house!"
Speaker B: "Shit, you've let the dog in the house!"

I am sure you will discover that most of them will identify speaker A as female and speaker B as male. In addition, these individuals will agree that hard and soft core obscenities are also characteristic of male talk. Accordingly, even our selection of expletives is determined by our sex role.

It should be noted that while women are using stronger expletives than in the past—an indication, according to Lakoff, of psychological liberation—most Americans still disapprove of females adopting them. That is, because women in America are still expected to be passive, docile, and sexually naive, it is not surprising that they are supposed to avoid emotionally charged expletives, particularly those dealing with sexuality (i.e., obscenity).

Sex roles, then, are also responsible for well-defined, predictable language patterns. For once we know an individual's gender, we can often predict what adjectives and expletives the speaker will use. Similarly, gender also influences body language in predictable ways. To examine the nonverbal dimension, join me for a walk down the avenue.

Trucking on Down the Avenue

Watch just about any female walk down the street and you will immediately notice the gender's most identifiable nonverbal idiosyncracy. The wiggle or sway, a rolling of the pelvis from side to side, has been a female trademark from time immemorial. Some males find this behavior so provocative that they have been known to gape, whistle, even cry out at the sight of a female pelvis in motion.

Though many people are convinced that the pelvic sway stems from biological differences between men and women, Ray Birdwhistell argues that it is just another acquired sex role behavior.[8] That is, while men and women are physically capable of rolling their hips, only females are encouraged to do it. Furthermore, men that wiggle too much compromise their masculinity and are often considered homosexual. Traditionally a characteristic of females, the sway is an example of what Birdwhistell calls *gender display*—socially accepted nonverbal behavior of men and women.

Males and females also differ substantially in the way they use their eyes. Certainly, we are all familiar with the ogling male staring conspicuously at a passing female. A nonverbal display of masculinity, men are permitted, even encouraged, to indiscretely eye a woman from head to toe.

Females, however, are not as fortunate as men for they must refrain from boldly examining the male anatomy. In fact, a woman who looks searchingly at a passing man may be considered sexually permissive. Unsurprisingly, female prostitutes often use wanton glances to communicate their intention to a potential customer. To avoid social censure, women have learned to use their eyes discretely, employing quick, inconspicuous glances to examine an unsuspecting male.

Predictability and Roles:
A Double-Edged Sword

The preceding section demonstrates that sex roles, like all social roles, make each communication encounter more predictable. Expecting those enacting a social role to communicate in certain ways, we are not as threatened by unfamiliar individuals for we already know something about them. As indicated earlier, however, these roles also narrow our behavioral options, forcing us to speak and act in a manner that may not be to our liking. It is this limitation that prompted the development of institutions founded on liberating people from traditional social roles.

UPSETTING THE COMMUNICATION
CART: ALTERNATIVE SOCIAL ROLES

With the appearance of many alternative institutions in the last decade, men and women were promised more freedom. Supposedly liberating their inhabitants from conventional sex role expectations, places like Sandstone encourage males and females to experiment with new communication styles. In these institutions, for example, women need not be passive and docile, compelled to display the verbal and nonverbal repertoire of femininity. Similarly, males can color their discourse with female adjectives, disclose deep feelings, and appear nonassertive without embarrassment.

Alternative institutions—be they communes, free schools, or open marriages—are not only concerned with gender roles. Communes, for example, are noted for shattering the traditional communication expectations of father, mother, and child. That is, since the care and responsibility of the home and children are shared by many people, daddy is no longer the only decision-maker; mommy is not the sole fountain of love and affection; and the kiddies are not compelled to be docile and obedient. Instead, individuals are permitted to enact social roles any way they desire.

Not only are family and sex roles undergoing change, but many individuals are taking a second look at work roles as well. Enlightened companies, for example, have instituted programs of "full disclosure" where employees are encouraged to speak candidly and express their feelings. Encouraged to develop this type of program by such organizational theorists as Herzberg, McGregor, and Trist—noted humanizers of the industrial setting—these institutions hope their disclosure plans will increase employee satisfaction and productivity.

Role Revolution: Boon or Bust?

Apparently, social roles are being seriously challenged in the United States. Whether this examination will ultimately result in more meaningful interpersonal encounters, increased personal happiness, and, in general, a more humane society is still unknown. We do know, however, that the role revolution is presently a mixed blessing, with obvious benefits and some deficiencies.

With respect to its shortcomings, the revolution has produced some new communication problems between men and women. With the advent of the women's movement, for example, men have had to carefully watch their language and behavior to avoid being labeled chauvinist. In fact, one study discovered that some men no longer know what topics to discuss with women or whether they should perform such male niceties as opening a door for a passing female.[9] In addition, though men realize women are becoming more assertive, sixty-five percent of the males interviewed in this study indicated that they would be "turned off" if an unfamiliar female approached them aggressively, asked for a date, and then took their phone number. It appears that many men still want to control male/female communication; in addition, others are experiencing a crisis in confidence in terms of topic and word choice.

The revolution in social roles is also responsible for communication difficulties at home and school. Desiring more individual freedom, youngsters, for example, are aggressively challenging authority figures. As kids become increasingly independent and assertive, it seems parents and teachers are finding it more difficult to communicate with them. Certainly, this communication breakdown is in part responsible for the rapidly growing number of teenagers who have run away from home and refuse to attend school.

In spite of these unfortunate problems, the revolution has also produced several positive changes in human communication. For instance, many marriages touched by the liberation movement have successfully redefined male and female roles, resulting in greater individual freedom for both husband and wife. In addition, studies on communes have found the male inhabitants more cooperative and empathetic than men in traditional institutions. Finally, for some families, the role revolution has opened channels of communication closed for years, thus bringing the members even closer together.

Free to be oneself, to speak and act as one chooses even while assuming a social role, is the primary objective of the liberation movement. With this in mind, you decide whether the revolution is worth the effort, whether it is potentially a boon or bust.

SUMMARY

1. A social role is an institutional position which places predictable behavioral demands on individuals.

   As members of many institutions—home, school, church, and the like—we play many social roles. Each demands certain verbal and nonverbal communication from us which we learn at an early age.

2. Through social conditioning and imitating others, we learn the communication expectations of each social role.

   We learn about social roles from our parents, the system's most effective social conditioners. In addition, by closely watching the behavior of others, we discover what is expected of us when enacting a social role.

3. Interpersonal misunderstandings, even conflict, may result when communication expectations are violated.

   We expect individuals playing a social role to communicate in certain ways. Naturally, those who violate these verbal and nonverbal expectations cause interpersonal tension. This type of stress often culminates in hostility and conflict.

4. Social roles can be psychologically and communicatively destructive.

   It has been shown that social roles often alienate people from themselves and others. This is particularly true of sex roles since they frequently prevent men and women from ever knowing one another.

5. Role contamination severely hampers human communication.

   Communicating role to role rather than person to person is role contamination. Though common, this type of interaction can be most ineffective. Hence, individuals should strive to touch the human being living within each social role.

6. Interrole conflict produces psychological and interpersonal tension, often weakening a human relationship.

This problem occurs when the communication expectations of two or more roles conflict. It was demonstrated that interrole conflict can impair communication, thereby debilitating the relationship.

7. Social roles and their attendant communication expectations are being seriously challenged in the United States.
Alternative institutions are dedicated to liberating people from traditional social roles. Though they presently appear to be a mixed blessing, these alternatives, a manifestation of a widespread role revolution, may ultimately be instrumental in humanizing society.

PRACTICE CASE STUDY

Born and raised in the North, Dr. Brown, a noted black psychiatrist, attended an all-black university in Alabama while training to be a physician. As a student in this unfamiliar region, Dr. Brown discovered that the South was substantially different than the North, particularly in its treatment of black people. In fact, after his first experience with a "redneck," the aspiring physician almost quit medical school and returned home. Let's return to that moment.

Exhausted from studying for exams, this struggling graduate student and his wife decided one weekend to visit some historical sites in Alabama. So they started up their old Chrysler and took off for Birmingham.

Shortly after they entered the expressway, the Browns were stopped by the State Patrol. Quite certain he had not violated any traffic law, the student waited for the white policeman to approach his car.

"Hey boy," observed the burly officer, "don't you know the speed limit?"

"Officer, according to my speedometer, I was actually traveling well below the speed limit," Brown explained. "In addition, sir, as you can plainly see, I'm no boy."

And with that the officer suddenly opened the car door, grabbed Mr. Brown's arm, and pulled him out of the automobile. Having observed the incident, the officer's partner rushed from the patrol car, gun in hand. And Mrs. Brown, a shy, quiet woman, went to her husband's assistance.

"Look boy," repeated the arresting officer, "I said you were speeding! You be a respectful nigger now or you'll wish you were never born. I don't want no uppity nigger talk from you!"

Trying desperately to contain his anger, Mr. Brown, turning

briefly to his wife as though asking for forgiveness, addressed the enraged patrolman.

"I is sorry for making trouble for ya'll. I don't read all dat well. I guess I just done gone a bit too fast. I hopes ya'll ain't too angry wit dis po' nigger."

Smiling broadly, the officer issued a traffic citation to Brown as his partner returned to the patrol car. Thanking him for the unwarranted ticket, Brown slowly entered his car. Deep in thought, he gazed out the window.

EXPLORATORY QUESTIONS

1. Initially, was Dr. Brown's enacted role of a southern black man substantially different from the expectations of the white officer? Refer to Chapter 9 for additional insights on the black person's role in the South.

2. Why do you think the officer became enraged with the way Dr. Brown communicated?

3. Why did Dr. Brown assume another communication style at the end of the encounter? What term would blacks use to describe this style (refer to Chapter 9)?

4. In what way were the several changes in the officer's demeanor linked to Dr. Brown's shifting communication style?

5. Was role contamination at all responsible for this communication breakdown? Similarly, on the basis of this case, what can be said about black/white communication and role contamination in the South?

6. Why did Dr. Brown look searchingly at his wife before changing his communication style at the end of the encounter? Do you think this had anything to do with interrole conflict?

7. Would you say that Dr. Brown's wife was in a potentially dangerous role conflict situation in terms of her own communication?

8. Was the ensuing conflict intensified because Dr. Brown and the officers were men?

9. In your opinion, how could this interpersonal conflict have been averted?

ADDITIONAL PROJECTS

1. Assuming that role contamination could have been avoided in the preceding encounter, rewrite the dialogue so that Dr. Brown

and the officer communicate person to person rather than role to role.

2. From what you know about black/white communication, extend the preceding case by including dialogue for the doctor's wife and the gun-toting officer. First speculate on their expected communication behavior and then consider other responses.

INTERPERSONAL COMMUNICATION EXERCISES

1. Social Roles and Communication: An Exercise
   An individual's communication is greatly influenced by social roles. To better understand this concept, participate in the following exercise.
   A. Find yourself a partner. Each of you is responsible for examining your partner's verbal and nonverbal behavior while he/she assumes two different social roles (i.e., student, daughter).
   B. After making these observations, share your perceptions with your partner.

2. Role Expectation Exercise
   To discover whether we really expect others to communicate in certain ways, try this exercise.
   A. Ask three people to describe how the following individuals normally behave. Have the interviewees list at least five descriptive adjectives for each person.
      1. Prostitute   6. Husband
      2. Priest   7. Wife
      3. Police officer 8. Middle-Aged Woman
      4. Lawyer   9. Professor
      5. Physician
   B. Discuss your findings with the class. What conclusions can be derived from this exercise?

3. Exercise on Sex Roles and Communication
   Have the communication patterns of males and females changed very much since the advent of the liberation movement? The following exercise should provide some insight into this question.
   A. Next time you're with several male/female couples closely observe the way they interact. Pay particular attention to the following:
      1. Who dominates the conversation, a male or a female?
      2. What do males talk about with one another?
      3. What do females talk about with one another?
      4. Do males and females use their respective "genderlects?"

5. Do males and females utilize appropriate gender displays?
B. Compare your findings with those of other class members. Would you conclude that the communication patterns of men and women have changed at all?

NOTES

[1] George Herbert Mead, *Mind, Self and Society* (University of Chicago Press, 1934).

[2] Jurgen Ruesch and Gregory Bateson, *Communication: The Social Matrix of Psychiatry* (New York: Norton, 1968).

[3] Sidney Jourard, *The Transparent Self* (New York: Van Nostrand, 1971), p. 30.

[4] Sidney Jourard and Paul Lasakow, "Some Factors in Self Disclosure," *Journal of Abnormal and Social Psychology*, vol. 56 (1958), pp. 91–98.

[5] Sidney Jourard, *The Transparent Self* (New York: Van Nostrand, 1971).

[6] Franklin Shaw, *Reconciliation: A Theory of Man Transcending* (New York: Van Nostrand, 1966).

[7] Robin Lakoff, "Language and Womans Place," *Language and Society*, vol. 2 (1973), p. 49.

[8] Ray Birdwhistell, *Kinesics and Context* (University of Pennsylvania Press, 1970).

[9] Robert Shuter, "Male/Female Interaction," Marquette University, 1976 (unpublished manuscript).

Understanding Misunderstandings: Practicing What's Been Preached

"I can't talk to my mother!"
"My girlfriend just doesn't understand me!"
"My husband never listens to me!"

Communication problems; we experience at least one every day. Plagued by interpersonal difficulties, we reach out for help to a wide variety of individuals: counselors, bartenders, teachers, taxi drivers, and friends. In desperation, we may write Dear Abby about our problems only to discover that she may not have any answers. On occasion, we may attempt to resolve a misunderstanding by consulting the people who know us best—ourselves. We could solve many of our interpersonal hassles if we only carefully examined them.

Dedicated to those of you who would like to avoid and reconcile daily communication breakdowns, this chapter demonstrates how you can use the contents of this book to achieve this goal.

LEARNING FROM THE PAST: COMMUNICATION HINDSIGHT

About to leave the hospital after taking a series of chest X-rays, Kim, a college sophomore, overheard her doctor talking to the radiologist.

"How old is Kim?" the radiologist inquired.

"Only twenty years old," her doctor responded.

"Ah ha, I see," the radiologist coldly snapped.

Unable to hear them anymore, Kim rushed to the telephone and called her boyfriend. Panic stricken, she sobbed,

"You should've heard those doctors talking about me, Tom. From what they said, you'd think I had cancer or something!"

You guessed it; Kim did not have cancer. In fact, her X-rays were perfectly normal. Why did she misunderstand the doctors' conversation? Read Kim's explanation which appeared in a diary prepared for my interpersonal communication class.

"My attitudes got the best of me. That is, I thought for sure something was wrong with me when I went to the hospital for tests. When I heard the doctors talking about me, I naturally thought the worst because I believed I was sick. My interpretation of their words and tone of voice was governed by my attitudes."

A bright student, Kim correctly applied the material in Chapter 3 to one of her past misunderstandings. After analyzing the encounter, Kim better understood what caused the breakdown and also discovered that she is quite capable of misunderstanding information. In the future, Kim may interpret messages more cautiously.

Like Kim, each of us can learn from our past misunderstandings if we just take the time to explore them. How do we examine an interaction that has already occurred? Let's find out.

EXAMINING A PAST ENCOUNTER: THE THREE-STEP COMMUNICATION ANALYSIS (T.S.C.A.)

You've just had a big argument with your beloved. Angry and frustrated, you storm out of his/her house, jump into your car, and high-tail it to the local pub. While sipping some brew, your mind wanders to the battle. Why did it happen?

To analyze a past encounter, you can use the Three-Step Communication Analysis which consists of the following stages: isolation, identification, and implication.

In the first step, isolation, you try to recall the many undesirable behaviors that you and your partner(s) displayed. For example, the two of you may have engaged in physical abuse, screamed at each other, and called each other names. Once the undesirable behaviors are isolated, you can proceed to step two (identification) in order to determine why you and your partner(s) behaved this way.

During the identification step, the causes of both the misunderstanding and undesirable behaviors are identified. To accomplish this, you should systematically analyze the encounter with the contents of this book. Derived from Chapters 1 through 10, the following probe questions should assist you in conducting your analysis.

Communication Risks and Rituals

1. Did the communicators engage in focused and/or unfocused interaction? What effect did this have on the encounter?
2. Was the interaction synchronized or unsynchronized? How did this influence the transaction?
3. Did either communicator have a low self-concept? In what way did this affect the interaction?
4. Was either communicator reluctant to disclose thoughts and feelings? Did this contribute to the misunderstanding?

Perception

5. Was selective perception at all responsible for the misunderstanding? What part did gender and attitudes play in selective perception?
6. Did the communicators' attitudes and backgrounds affect their interpretation of a message?

Verbal and Nonverbal Communication

7. Did the communicators misunderstand one another's words?
8. Did the communicators use devil terms and/or violate verbal taboos? Were these terms partly responsible for the misunderstanding?
9. Did either communicator monopolize the conversation? How did this affect the interaction?
10. Did either communicator touch his/her partner(s) too much or too little? How did this affect the encounter?
11. Were the communicators confused by one another's gestures, postures, and facial expressions?
12. Did the communicators misunderstand each other's proxemic orientation?
13. Were the communicators' paralinguistic cues at all responsible for the misunderstandings?

Interpersonal Games and Conflict

14. Did the communicators engage in impression management? How did this affect the interaction?

15. Did the communicators play any head or con games? Was game playing partly responsible for the misunderstanding?
16. Did the communicators interact defensively? How did this affect the transaction?
17. Were the communicators competing with one another? Did this produce interpersonal hostility?
18. Did domination, misperception, and/or distrust lead to hostility?

Social Context, Subculture, and Roles

19. Was a situational propriety violated during the encounter? What effect did this have on the interaction?
20. Did the communicators have stereotypes of one another? How did this affect the transmission of information?
21. Was either communicator using a sublanguage? Did this contribute to the misunderstanding?
22. Were the communicators from different cultures? Did this affect the way they interacted?
23. Did either communicator violate role expectations? In what way was the encounter influenced by this?
24. Were role contamination and/or interrole conflict responsible for the misunderstanding?

If you answer each probe question, you should be able to identify the cause(s) of a communication problem. For example, after analyzing the preceding conflict with your beloved, you may discover that the two of you have been competing excessively with each other, a source of hostility for many couples. You may also learn that both of you engaged in defensive interaction which only intensified the confrontation. With this information, you and your partner have a better chance of avoiding similar battles in the future, which brings us to step three.

In the implication phase (step three), you reexamine what caused a misunderstanding and decide how to avert this type of problem in the future. For instance, you may conclude that you and your sweetheart have to stop competing with each other, once you have identified competition as the cause of a previous row. In addition, if you discovered that defensive communication aggravated a past conflict with your beloved, you may decide to fight fairly with him/her in the future. An important step, the implication phase encourages you to learn from your past mistakes.

With the Three-Step Communication Analysis, you can also analyze an interaction in which you did *not* participate. To do this, you need a detailed description of the misunderstanding from participants and/or witnesses. If you secure sufficient information, you should be able to (1) isolate the parties' negative behaviors (isolation step), (2) determine what caused these behaviors and the attendant misunderstanding (identification step), and (3) suggest how the parties involved could avoid a similar problem in the future (implication step).

Does the Three-Step Communication Analysis sound complicated? It's really quite easy to use. To demonstrate this, the following case is examined vis-a-vis the Three-Step Communication Analysis.

BAGELS AND WHITE BREAD: USING T.S.C.A.

Twenty-one years old and madly in love, Harriet White, a Protestant college student, has decided to introduce her boyfriend to mom and dad when she visits them on Christmas vacation. It was a tough decision to make, since she knows her parents do not care for Jews, and her boyfriend just happens to be one. To lessen the shock, Harriet called her mother and delicately disclosed that Paul was Jewish; mom was definitely upset. Aware of Mr. and Mrs. White's attitudes toward Jews, Paul was not looking forward to visiting them.

On arriving home, Harriet and Paul were greeted quite warmly by the Whites. "What an act," Paul thought. "They are as phony as a three dollar bill; I just don't trust them."

After inviting the group into the living room, Mr. White approached Paul. "So tell me, Paul, what are you studying at school, accounting, advertising, marketing? I know you people are interested in making money any way you can."

"On the contrary Mr. White, we people are interested in quite a few things," Paul responded sarcastically. "For example, I'm majoring in philosophy."

Annoyed by Paul's tone of voice, Mr. White quickly retorted. "What do you intend to do when you graduate college? Be a philosopher?"

Sensing that Paul and her father were not getting along, Harriet interrupted the conversation and changed the subject. Mr. White and Paul avoided each other for the remainder of the vacation.

CASE ANALYSIS. The preceding case happened to a close friend of mine who provided the details. To find out why Mr. White and Paul did not hit it off, let's use the Three-Step Communication Analysis.

Step One: Isolation. Both Paul and Mr. White communicated inappropriately. First, Mr. White's words were poorly chosen; in fact, he insulted Paul when he said "you people are interested in making money any way you can." Paul's sarcastic response to Mr. White's statement only made matters worse. Finally, Mr. White's tactless assault on Paul's academic major was certainly unnecessary.

Step Two: Identification. Why did Paul and Mr. White communicate in the preceding ways? Relying on information provided in the case study, I was able to answer many of the probe questions and identify several possible reasons for the characters' undesirable behaviors.

For instance, while examining probe question 6, I discovered that the communicators' attitudes prevented them from interacting effectively. In Mr. White's case, he believes that Jews are sly and mercenary; accordingly, he naturally assumed Paul wanted to be a greedy businessman. Mr. White's attitudes about Jews were so deeply ingrained that he could not understand why Paul resented being characterized this way.

Similarly, Paul's responses were also influenced by his attitudes about the Whites. For example, since Paul had an unfavorable opinion of Mr. and Mrs. White before he ever met them, it is not surprising he thought their warm greeting was "as phony as a three dollar bill." In addition, Paul *expected* Mr. White to slander Jews; that's why he *overreacted* to Mr. White's foolish, though harmless statement about Jewish interest in money.

Finally, in answering probe question 16, we discover that the confrontation escalated in intensity because the participants communicated defensively. Upset by Mr. White's ethnic slur, Paul, for example, went on the offensive and used sarcasm to belittle his opponent. In turn, Mr. White attacked Paul's academic major which also increased hostility. Preoccupied with verbally assaulting each other, neither communicator wanted to resolve their differences.

Step Three: Implication. If Paul and Mr. White ever speak again, they have to communicate quite differently to avert another battle. For starters, Mr. White must refrain from making anti-Semitic statements, a goal that can be achieved once he realizes that his attitudes about Jews are reflected in his language.

Furthermore, in case of future conflict between the communicators, they should fight fairly; insults and sarcasm only complicate matters. In fact, before Paul and Mr. White can begin ironing out their interpersonal problems, they must stop communicating defensively.

Now do you see how the Three-Step Communication Analysis can help you better understand a past encounter? Moreover, T.S.C.A. can also be used to analyze an interaction *while* it is taking place. Consider.

EXAMINING AN INTERACTION IN PROGRESS: T.S.C.A. TO THE RESCUE

While eating at a restaurant, I spotted Daryl Smile, Mr. Popularity from my high school class. Interested in finding out whether he became an all-American success, I sauntered over to his table.

"Hi, Daryl, long time no see."

Mouth full, dimpled Daryl loudly exclaimed in his inimitable style, "Hey, I remember that ugly face. It's Bob four-eyes from Beaver High. How's the queer of the senior class doing these days?"

Embarrassed by his remarks, I felt like letting Daryl have it; instead, I quickly analyzed the situation and ventilated my feelings descriptively.

"Daryl you needn't insult me; I just came over to say hello. I don't know why you feel compelled to put me down. Does it make you feel superior?"

Stunned by my disclosure, Daryl suddenly became more pleasant; the Three-Step Communication Analysis had worked.

How did I turn this hostile confrontation into a reasonably effective encounter? I used an abbreviated version of T.S.C.A. to analyze my partner's communication as well as my own.

Though I did not have time to thoroughly examine each step of the communication analysis, I was able to (1) isolate the words and actions that offended me, (2) identify these behaviors as negative evaluation and superiority, two types of defensive communication, and (3) suggest that Daryl stop interacting this way. When I ventilated my feelings descriptively, a fair fighting technique discussed in Chapter 7, Daryl treated me more humanely.

As demonstrated in this case, you can actually utilize the Three-Step Communication Analysis *during* an encounter to improve interpersonal interaction. To accomplish this, you need to be sensitive to the way you and your partner(s) are communicating. With this heightened sensitivity, you can quickly discover:

1. if you or your partner is interacting inappropriately (isolation step);

2. what caused you or your partner to communicate this way (identification step);

3. what you and your partner should say and do to improve the transaction (implication step).

Since you will not have time to consult the probe questions included in the identification step, you must have a thorough understanding of the contents of this book to determine what caused the misunderstanding. You will then know what has to be said and done to improve communication (implication step) after you have analyzed the encounter.

The Three-Step Communication Analysis: Postscript

QUESTION: Will the Three-Step Communication Analysis solve all my communication problems?

ANSWER: Not on your life.

What T.S.C.A. should do, however, is help you better understand your daily misunderstandings, certainly a valuable insight. Whether you use this information to prevent and resolve communication hassles is up to you.

NEW WORLD COMIN'?

"There's a new world comin'
just around the bend.
I said, a new world comin';
this one has got to come to an end.
I hear a new voice calling;
the one we had visions of.
Coming in peace,
Coming in love,
Coming in joy."

("New World Comin'," Barry Mann and Cynthia Weil, Screen Gems: EMI Music Inc. Reprinted by Permission)

Is a new world really coming—a world of honesty, sensitivity, understanding, and concern? It depends on you and me, along with everyone else on this planet.

We could usher in a new world if only we took a second look at the way we communicate. In so doing, we might discover that we play games quite a bit, intimidate and insult people too often, listen more to ourselves than others, misinterpret messages at every turn, stereotype neighbors and friends, dominate our loved ones, compete excessively, monopolize conversations . . . ad infinitum. Knowing this, we can try to change our behavior and strive to become the best possible communicators—supportive, sensitive, and understanding.

So you see, a new world is possible. It's up to you and me.

SUMMARY

1. Individuals can learn from their past misunderstandings if only they took the time to analyze them.

   In examining a past misunderstanding, the Three-Step Communication Analysis (T.S.C.A.) can be used. Consisting of three phases—isolation, identification, and implication—T.S.C.A. can make misunderstandings understandable.

2. In T.S.C.A., each step has a specific function.

   In the first step (isolation), the communicator tries to recall the many undesirable behaviors that were displayed. During the identification step, the causes of both the misunderstanding and undesirable behaviors are identified. Finally, the communicator decides how to avert this type of problem in the future, the implication step.

3. With the Three-Step Communication Analysis, individuals can analyze an interaction in which they did not participate.

   To accomplish this, an individual needs a detailed description of the misunderstanding from participants and/or witnesses. With sufficient information, each step in T.S.C.A. can be examined.

4. Communicators can use T.S.C.A. to analyze an interaction *while* it is taking place.

   To utilize T.S.C.A. during an encounter, communicators must be sensitive to their own communication style and that of their partner. With this heightened sensitivity, communicators should be able to isolate a communication problem, identify its causes, and remedy the difficulty.

5. A new world is possible; it's up to all of us.

   As communicators, we all have our faults. If each of us would try to become the best possible communicators, this planet would be a much better place in which to live.

PRACTICE CASE STUDIES

Use the Three-Step Communication Analysis to analyze the following case studies.

Case One

For Paul Williams, a college junior, university life is miserable; he can't stand his roommate, Sidney. The two of them used to get along until old Sid spotted Paul's girlfriend, Barbara Hanson. In the heat of passion, Sid called Barbara for a date; she didn't accept, but Paul found out.

The relationship worsened when Paul accused Sid of stealing his wristwatch. Paul was certain his roommate had lifted the expensive watch; no one else was sneaky enough to do it. No wonder Paul was surprised to learn that the watch was at his mother's house. He had accidentally left it there.

Then there was the fight they had over cleaning up their room; Paul and Sid viciously attacked each other. After the confrontation, Paul started a rumor that Sid was an alcoholic; the two rarely spoke again.

Case Two

While sitting in my office, I was visited by Dave, a student in one of my classes. Visibly disturbed, Dave sadly explained why he hadn't been in class for the last four weeks.

"My mother is very sick," he tearfully confessed. "I've been home taking care of her."

Feeling sure I had seen Dave a week earlier playing basketball in the school gym, I asked him about it and he nervously responded, "Dr. Shuter, I got back to campus last week but just couldn't go back to class; I was too upset. Basketball was about the only thing I could do to relieve my anxieties." Beginning to weep, Dave added, "I know you understand how I feel, Dr. Shuter. After all, you're a parent."

Touched by Dave's childlike demeanor, I found myself consoling him, as though he was my son. Grateful for my reaction Dave said, "Dr. Shuter, you're really a good person. Those kids of yours are really lucky to have a father like you." After hearing that remark, I excused him for being absent and even agreed to tutor him.

While talking to a colleague a few days later, I discovered quite accidentally that Dave had attended his class for the last four weeks. I had been conned.

Case Three

A cosmopolitan city, San Francisco attracts tourists from throughout the world. With people interacting from numerous cultures, it is not surprising that communication problems sometimes occur in the city by the bay.

On one occasion, I was riding on a crowded cable car waiting for the conductor to collect my fare. As he neared me, I noticed him requesting the twenty-five-cent tariff from a Japanese woman. Unable to speak English, the passenger gave the conductor a dollar, though the fare was to be paid with exact change.

"Lady, I need a quarter," the burly conductor observed. Confused by the request, the woman smiled at the conductor.

"Look lady, I don't want your smiles; I want a quarter."

Frustrated, the conductor turned to another passenger for the fare when suddenly the Japanese woman cried out to him. "Money— I want money." Apparently, she knew the fare was only a quarter but did not understand what exact change was.

"If you want to stay on this car," the conductor bellowed angrily, "I'll have to keep your dollar; I can't give you change." With that, he turned his back on the woman.

Still smiling, the Japanese passenger got up, grabbed the conduc-

tor from behind, and howled repeatedly, "Money, give me; money, give me."
The remaining passengers looked on in disbelief.

SELECTED BIBLIOGRAPHY

Getting Acquainted with Interpersonal Communication

1. Barnland, Dean, *Interpersonal Communication: Survey and Studies.* New York: Houghton Mifflin, 1968.
2. Berlo, David, *The Process of Communication.* New York: Holt, Rinehart and Winston, 1960.
3. Giffin, Kim, and Patton, Bobby, *Fundamentals of Interpersonal Communication.* New York: Harper & Row, 1971.
4. Johnson, David, *Reaching Out: Interpersonal Effectiveness and Self-Actualization.* Englewood Cliffs, N.J.: Prentice-Hall, 1972.
5. Keltner, John, *Interpersonal Speech-Communication: Elements and Structure.* Belmont, Ca.: Wadsworth, 1970.
6. Stewart, John, Ed., *Bridges Not Walls.* Reading, Mass.: Addison-Wesley, 1973.
7. Villard, Kenneth, and Whipple, Leland, *Beginnings in Relational Communication.* New York: Wiley, 1976.

More on Verbal Communication

1. Brown, Charles, and Van Riper, Charles, *Speech and Man.* Englewood Cliffs, N.J.: Prentice-Hall, 1966.
2. Chase, Stuart, *The Tyranny of Words.* New York: Harcourt Brace Jovanovich, 1953.
3. Dale, Philip, *Language Development, Structure and Function.* Hinsdale, Il.: Dryden Press, 1972.
4. Korzbski, Alfred, *Selections from Science and Sanity.* Lakeville, Conn.: The International Nonaristotelian Library Publishing Company, 1948.
5. Lee, Irving, *Language Habits in Human Affairs.* New York: Harper & Row, 1941.

Reading About Nonverbal Communication

1. Harrison, Randall, *Beyond Words: An Introduction to Nonverbal Communication.* Englewood Cliffs, N.J.: Prentice-Hall, 1975.
2. Knapp, Mark, *Nonverbal Communication in Human Interaction.* New York: Holt, Rinehart and Winston, 1972.
3. Mehrabian, Albert, *Silent Messages.* Belmont, Ca.: Wadsworth, 1971.
4. Scheflen, Albert, *Body Language and Social Order: Communication as Behavioral Control.* Englewood Cliffs, N.J.: Prentice-Hall. 1972.
5. Sommer, Robert, *Personal Space.* Englewood Cliffs, N.J.: Prentice-Hall, 1969.

Exploring Manipulation and Conflict

1. Deutch, Morton, "Conflicts: Production and Destruction," *Journal of Social Issues*, vol. 25, 1969.
3. Rogers, Carl, *Becoming Partners: Marriage and its Alternatives*. New York: Dell, 1972.
4. Satir, Virginia, *Peoplemaking*. Palo Alto, Ca.: Science and Behavior Books, 1972.
5. Shoestrum, Everett, *Man: The Manipulator*. New York: Abingdon Press, 1967.

Reflecting on Culture and Communication

1. Allport, Gordon, *The Nature of Prejudice*. Reading, Mass.: Addison-Wesley, 1954.
2. Kochman, Thomas, *Rappin' and Stylin' Out: Communication in Urban Black America*. University of Illinois Press, 1972.
3. Liebow, Elliott, *Tally's Corner*. New York: Little, Brown, 1967.
4. Rich, Andrea, *Interracial Communication*. New York: Harper & Row, 1974.
5. Whyte, William, *Street Corner Society: The Social Structure of an Italian Slum*. University of Chicago Press, 1943.

Social Roles: Additional Insights

1. Allport, Gordon, *Becoming*. New Haven, Conn.: Yale University Press, 1955.
2. Bugental, John, *The Search for Authenticity*. New York: Holt, Rinehart and Winston, 1965.
3. Fromm, Eric, *Man for Himself*. New York: Holt, Rinehart and Winston, 1947.
4. Jourard, Sidney, *Disclosing Man to Himself*. Princeton: Van Nostrand, 1968.
5. Laing, R. D., *The Self and Others*. Chicago: Quadrangle, 1962.

Index